THE PURSUIT OF THE GOOD LIFE

THE PURSUIT

OF THE

GOOD LIFE

TED HAGGARD

Charisma
HOUSE
A STRANG COMPANY

Most STRANG COMMUNICATIONS/CHARISMA HOUSE/SILOAM/REALMS products are available at special quantity discounts for bulk purchase for sales promotions, premiums, fund-raising, and educational needs. For details, write Strang Communications/Charisma House/Siloam/Realms, 600 Rinehart Road, Lake Mary, Florida 32746, or telephone (407) 333-0600.

THE PURSUIT OF THE GOOD LIFE by Ted Haggard
Published by Charisma House
A Strang Company
600 Rinehart Road
Lake Mary, Florida 32746
www.charismahouse.com

Unless otherwise noted, all Scripture quotations are from the Holy Bible, New International Version. Copyright © 1973, 1978, 1984, International Bible Society. Used by permission.

Cover design by Judith McKittrick

Library of Congress Cataloging-in-Publication Data
Haggard, Ted.
  The pursuit of the good life / Ted Haggard.
    p. cm.
  ISBN 1-59185-996-4 (hard back)
  1. Christian life. I. Title.
  BV4501.3.H3455 2006
  248.4--dc22
                                        2006011343
First Edition

06 07 08 09 10 — 987654321
Printed in the United States of America

This book is dedicated to one of my dearest friends, Patton Dodd, who lives the good life. Patton is everything I describe in this book. I trust him, I depend upon him, and I immensely value him because of the life he has found in Christ.

Contents

Part One

How to Pursue the Good Life

There is no tabernacle any longer. But the items contained within it can speak to us today about how to approach God, be in relationship with Him, and know our purpose in life.

CHAPTER ONE

The Good News of the Good Life

Y ou are reading this sentence for a reason.

It is no accident that you picked up this book and let your eyes fall upon these words.

Your life is not ruled by chance. Your life is not a whim. It has purpose.

There is something specific for you in these pages. The strategies contained herein will lead you to the good life—a life that makes sense, a life that works, a life that brims with confidence, connectivity, and competence.

Do I have all the answers for you? No. *I* don't. But I do know where to find the answers, and I'll take you there.

As you read this book, you will take a journey through the stages that lead to a life of success. You will learn how to deal with your past, how to settle yourself in the present, and how to move forward with clarity into a better future. You will learn your reason for living. You will learn how to put one foot in front of the other with your head held high, your eyes focused, and your heart filled with assurance that you are moving in the right direction.

You can do well. You can win. You can live the good life.

In fact, I believe you were *designed* for the good life. You are here for a specific purpose, and as you learn that purpose, the door to the good life will be opened for you.

What the Good Life Is

I have used the phrase four times already—*the good life*. In order to pursue it, we have to know what it is. I will define it, explain it, and tell stories about it throughout the course of this book, but for now, I will give you three of the key ideas. To me, the good life is about:

- *Confidence.* So many people today are plagued by uncertainty. They are not sure *who* they are, *why* they are, or *what* their lives are for. They lack that gut-level assurance that says, "Yes! This is the right direction for me. This is who I am. This is what I am supposed to do." In the good life, we can have confidence in every area of life. We can trust and know. From working in our jobs to raising our kids to spending our resources, we can act with strength and security that *this is right for me. This is what I should be doing.* The good life helps us find that confidence.

- *Connectivity.* Most of us are surrounded by people most of our lives—family, friends, or even just co-workers and associates—but many of us do not manage to connect. All the heart stuff that goes with relationships—which is admittedly messy sometimes—is crucial to living the good life. We were not made to be alone; humans are designed to be in relationship with one another. In the good life, we learn to connect with wis-

dom, honesty, transparency, discretion, gracious-
ness, affection, and love.

- *Competence.* This is one of my favorite concepts,
  and I have tucked a full discussion of it into the
  final chapters of this book. Competence is a
  description of complete living; it's doing life well.
  It's becoming your best self. It's treating others
  right and not descending into hurt and frustration. It's reading great books and understanding
  big ideas. It's assurance. It's holding your head
  high and articulating clearly. It's achieving a balance between trusting that God knows what He
  is doing and being responsible to do your part.
  It's living the good life day in, day out.

But the good life is more than confidence, connectivity, and
competence—it is many other things that don't even begin with
the letter *c*! As you turn the pages of this book, you will read
about true faith, forgiveness, and hope. You will read about how
to treat other people and how to react to people who might not
treat you so well. You will read about how to understand the God
who made you and how to know what He thinks about you. You
will read about dealing with your yesterday and preparing for your
tomorrow.

In short, you will read about the good news of the good life.
And more than that, you will begin living it.

How the Big Questions Make Life Make Sense

Every good book answers a big question, or several big questions.
As we begin the journey to the good life, it is important to know
which questions we are trying to answer.

It is my hope that our discussion of the good life will answer
lots of questions. The more we live the good life, the more we

know the answers to questions people are asking about relating to people, spending money, raising kids, choosing jobs, dealing with religion, understanding politics, and more. But to frame things here, let's narrow it down to two, or two types of, questions that need answering in order for us to live the good life.

> *If we know who God is and what He is like, we know a lot about our purpose in life. If we know what He expects from us, we know a lot about how to live.*

The first is about God's relationship to me. What does God have to do with my life? Like you, I have wondered a lot about this. What is His responsibility to me? Where is He? What is He doing? And how is He involved in what I think and do? Is He evaluating me, or has He already decided what He is going to do with me—both now and for eternity?

The second is a mirror of the first. What does my life have to do with God? What is my responsibility to Him? How much does what I do and who I am matter to Him? How much difference do I make, and do my actions really affect anything? Consequences. Cause and effect. Does what I do matter at all? How much importance does my life have? And even if I can make some small imprint in some small way on this earth, what happens after? Does eternity depend on what I do now, or is the future already decided?

Another way of saying all this is to put it into one big question: *How much of my life is up to God, and how much of it is up to me?*

To some, these might seem like abstract questions people ask when they are thinking about religion or philosophy. But think about it for a moment, and you will see how pressing and urgent these questions are. If we know who God is and what He is like, we know a lot about our purpose in life. If we know what He expects from us, we know a lot about how to live.

If we never determine the answers to these questions, then we might make up life as we go. We will never really be focused, never really settled and moving in a positive direction.

But in the good life, we are. We have answers to the big questions. We have tracks to run on. The good life makes life make sense.

Have you ever noticed a red-tailed hawk dive for its prey? It is a majestic sight. The bird soars gracefully in the sky, and as you watch it, you begin to think it is just randomly floating and enjoying its flight. The hawk does not look focused—it looks as if it is hovering because hovering is fun. Sometimes it flies so high you can barely see it from the ground. It is a mesmerizing, trancelike float.

But suddenly, in a flash, the hawk dips its beak toward the ground and dives straight down until only a few inches from the ground, swooping back up after it has captured its prey.

And then it is clear—the hawk wasn't randomly flying at all. It wasn't hovering just to hover. It was focused on something, and it knew how to get it.

That's what I mean when I talk about the good life. It makes us hawk-like. It is the opposite of a haphazard, unfocused, and arbitrary existence. But the good life is so satisfying and enjoyable that, to others, we might look as if we are just going with the flow and randomly pursuing the opportunities that come our way. And sure enough, sometimes we can just spread our wings and enjoy the flight. But we are focused. We are determined. We are in sync. And when the moment is right, we know how to act.

Want it? It's yours. Everything has been set up for you. There is a journey, a road to walk. You might even be further along than you think. Whether that's the case or you are just starting out, this book will give you a map. You will know where you have been, where you are now, and where you need to be.

You will know how to find the good life and how to make sure the rest of your life truly is good.

CHAPTER TWO

The Good Story: What God Wants You to Know

As a boy growing up in a small town in Indiana, I would lie in our yard at night and stare at the constellations and all the twinkling lights in the sky—all those stars, planets, planes, satellites, and occasional streaks of lights indicating that another chunk of space just entered Earth's atmosphere.

I thought that every glimmer of distant light validated that there was a Creator. As a kid enjoying a rural childhood, I knew that trees, water, blue skies, clouds, and brisk nights could not have just formed randomly. I was convinced that someone, somewhere had a plan. Leaves and seasons were too special, evening breezes were too wonderful, and summer showers were too refreshing to be arbitrary. Some Life had to be behind life.

There was a purpose to everything. And sometimes, I wondered if that purpose was...*me.*

Don't all kids wonder if they are the center of the universe? I know I did. *Could it be,* I thought, *that everything only exists when I am there? Could it be that everything just exists for my pleasure?*

Understand, I was only six. I was trying to determine if maybe, just maybe, I was the only one alive, and if everything else and everyone else was an illusion placed here to entertain me.

Was I self-centered? Of course. But I was trying to find a reason for it all, and like many people (many of who are *much* older than six), I was clutching for an answer. I was also learning to love the adventure and mystery of life.

When I grew up, I saw that adults ask the same questions, often without answers any more conclusive than those I had as a little boy on an Indiana farm. The difference is that adults have education, semantics, the benefit of history, and influence. As adults, we can create institutions to probe the galaxies. We can start new philosophical systems. We can propose esoteric theories and make people feel ignorant for not understanding them. We can spend billions of dollars on pursuing every mystery of our existence. We do all those things, and many of them are good. Yet, all that work doesn't accomplish quite what it should. It doesn't necessarily make us better people. It often doesn't help us to know God or live the good life.

But it could. As we discover the mystery and complexity of the masterpiece within which we live, we should be motivated to pursue our purpose within creation. Our role is important. There is order in the universe, and there is an order for us. There is a story of the universe that we are slowly discovering. Maybe there is a story for us, too.

Humans have been telling stories for as long as they have been alive. Storytelling is among our oldest habits as a race. We know about ancient civilizations by what they have left behind, and often, what they have left behind is in story form—markings on papyrus, hieroglyphics, sculptures, and paintings that give us glimpses into their most deeply held beliefs.

In that grand tradition, I believe that God revealed Himself to us by telling us a story. He explained Himself and the purpose for all creation. Because of this story, we know our reason for being. Because of this story, we know how to live the best possible life.

You want to know best thing about God's story? We are all included in it. He did not leave us out of the narrative. We get to be characters, and we get to help write the ending. Each of our little stories fits into the one big story written by God.

The Story of All Stories

As you may know, among the five most-read books of all time are a collection of Jewish writings known as the Pentateuch (or the Torah)—Genesis, Exodus, Leviticus, Numbers, and Deuteronomy. They are the first five books of the Old Testament in the Bible. The books contain lots of information, but basically, the Pentateuch is an account of a man named Abraham who has an encounter with God. As a result of the encounter, Abraham's descendants through his son Isaac become a great nation known as Israel, and the Old Testament is a history of Israel's relationship with God.

If you have seen the front page of a newspaper lately, you know that Israel continues to be a nation of critical importance. Evangelical Christians, in particular, are very interested in their past, present, and future. Christians have an affinity for the Israeli people and their Scriptures because we know that God did, in fact, reveal Himself to the people of Israel and, later, extended the revelation to all humankind. We take Genesis, Exodus, and all the rest very seriously because we believe that the promises they contain are true for all of us.

We believe the stories in those books fold perfectly into the story of Jesus, who is God's Son and who Christians believe is the fulfillment of the promise to Abraham. In other words, Jesus provided the way for everyone on the earth to receive what God originally promised Abraham. (See Galatians 3:14.)

Jesus ministered to thousands of people during His lifetime on the earth, and we have very reliable records of His teachings. He was put to death by the authorities of His day, but He miraculously rose from the dead and ascended to heaven.

Now, hang with me here. I know many of you know this, but I have to frame the big ideas. We have to understand God's big story—the metanarrative—in order to grasp the story of our lives—the micronarrative.* The story of the Pentateuch, especially the part we are going to focus on in Exodus, is the beginning of the Story of all stories. It is the metanarrative for all creation. In this story, God reveals how we can be in relationship with Him.

In this story, God reveals how we can pursue the good life.

The tabernacle is going to be our key symbol as we discuss the pursuit of the good life....Through the detailed accounts of the tabernacle, God gave us a picture of the way to approach Him.

So, as we pursue the best possible life, we are going to talk about the Bible. We are going to deal with some history and pictures God gave us so we can see His plan for us. It sounds difficult, but really, it is very simple stuff. Stay with me, and you will see. The events recounted in one of the oldest stories in existence matter for you and me. Those ancient manuscripts contain words of wisdom, and they can change your life.

To start, let me give you the short version.

God created the world, including everything and everyone in it. He wanted to be in relationship with people, but people

---

*A *metanarrative* is a transcendent story, a larger-than-life narrative that explores big ideas and gives meaning. A *micronarrative* is a smaller story, often about an individual life.

rebelled against Him. So, as I mentioned, He revealed Himself to one man, Abraham, and made a covenant with Abraham to bless him, prosper him and his descendants, and to be in relationship with them forever. Later, some of Abraham's descendants became slaves in Egypt. God chose one man, named Moses, to liberate them. Moses did the job, and they escaped to the wilderness. There, they wandered and camped for several decades until settling in Canaan, the land originally promised to Abraham.

What I just said in one paragraph is a bird's-eye view of a narrative that is filled with layers and details. Often, people skip the technical material (otherwise known as "the second half of Exodus through Deuteronomy"), and it is not hard to see why. The Pentateuch is packed with minutiae about sacrificial offerings and ritual obligations and specifications about places of worship—down to the precise number of cubits. Seems like skippable stuff.

But one of those places, the tabernacle God instructed the Israelites to build in the wilderness, is something we cannot skip. In fact, this tabernacle is going to be our key symbol as we discuss the pursuit of the good life.

The Good Life Is in the Details

After God supernaturally helped the Jewish people escape from Egypt, He gave Moses several instructions about how the people could know Him. Among other things, He instructed them to build a place of worship where they could atone for their wrongdoings, receive forgiveness, and connect with the Creator. That place was the tabernacle—the place we are going to walk through as we learn to pursue the good life.

Why did God tell the Hebrews to build the tabernacle? Among other reasons, I believe it was so that He could give a message to every future generation. You see, the people in Moses' day depended upon Moses to hear from God and give them direction. They relied on his interaction with God to imbue their lives with purpose and goodness.

But God did not want people to be dependent upon a Moses of every generation. He wanted us to know how to know Him for ourselves. So, through the detailed accounts of the tabernacle, He gave us a picture of the way to approach Him. God told Moses how to build this structure in great detail, and the specifications we find inside it give us all we need to know God and pursue the best possible life.

The details of the story of the Hebrew tabernacle contain promises for you and me. If we read the details in the right light, we can unpack some of those promises. It is not hard to do. When I read about the Hebrew tabernacle, the life-giving ideas just leap off the page. They feed me, inspire me, and tell me my purpose. They give me the good life, and I want you to have it, too.

As you know, there is no tabernacle any longer. But the items contained within it can speak to us today about how to approach God, be in a relationship with Him, and know our purpose in life.

God knows why He created you.

He has a plan for your life.

And He has made it clear.

In order to know your purpose, in order to pursue a good life, you must first know your Creator on His terms. As you walk through the tabernacle, you can know, with absolute assurance, that you have approached God effectively. You will see clearly how God arranged for you to know Him personally, and you will find yourself walking into His perfect plan for your life.

Part Two

Entering Into the Good Life

Many Christians think the complete package God offers the church is a personal born-again experience in Christ, water baptism, and the filling of the Holy Spirit. That package is a wonderful, life-altering gift. But according to the symbolism of the tabernacle, there is much more.

CHAPTER THREE

The Good First Step: Where God Wants You to Go

Now that you know about the tabernacle, let's take the first step inside. But let's be careful about it. If we take this first step in the right way, we will be well on our way to living the good life.

Why is this first step so important, and why do we need to be so careful? Because we are talking about approaching God. To approach an authority figure, you have to understand protocol. If you were to meet with the president of the United States, you would enjoy greater success if you approached him according to established rules and customs. Actually, if you violated protocol, not only would his security personnel deny you access, but they also might actually arrest you or even kill you. At the highest levels of authority, protocol is that important.

God, of course, is the ultimate authority. And God has made the protocol for approaching Him clear. He has made a way for us to meet Him. But if we don't follow His way—if we refuse to ask directions or try to bushwhack our way to God—we could get sidetracked or even into serious trouble.

A Road Map to God

The tabernacle described in Exodus is a picture of the way God wants us to approach Him. Its various features, from the front door to the deepest room within, are a map of the journey to the good life in God.

Now, for the Israelites the tabernacle was more than a picture. It was a physical structure with enormous significance. It was their primary means of accessing the Creator.

During the time of the tabernacle, the Israelites were living in the wilderness. Moses was their leader because he had liberated them from slavery in Egypt. God gave Moses very specific instructions on how to build a place of worship for the Israelites. The details of this account can be found in Exodus 25–30, which we have reproduced in the appendix. You will be learning about the major details of this place of worship throughout the book, and I will explain the significance of each portion as we go. But I suggest you read the appendix if you are not familiar with the story.

Take a look at the drawing of the tabernacle on the facing page. Notice that it has three major "rooms": the outer court, the holy place, and the most holy place (also called the holy of holies). The outer court has two major pieces of furniture: the bronze altar and the bronze basin. The holy place has three items: a table with the bread of the presence, the lamp stand made of gold, and the altar of incense. The most holy place is guarded by a veil, and lying within it is the ark of the covenant.

For the Israelites, the tabernacle was a place of awe. They treated it with immense reverence, for it represented the very presence of God. They took it very seriously. Getting inside the tabernacle, and getting closer and closer to the holy place, meant getting very near the Creator of the universe and, more specifically, the God of Abraham. Actually, only priests could enter into the inner courts. And only the high priest could enter the most holy place—and

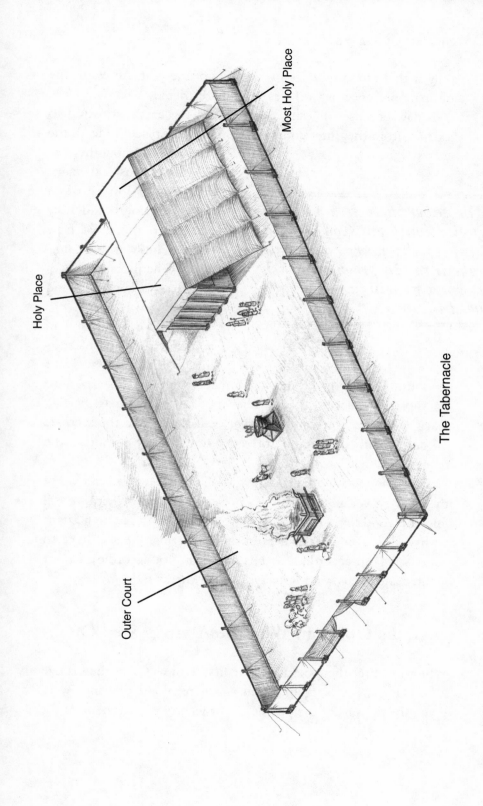

Most Holy Place

Holy Place

Outer Court

The Tabernacle

only with a blood sacrifice on one day of the year. Access to the ultimate presence of God was severely restricted.

Today, because of Jesus, everyone on the earth is invited to journey from the outer court to the most holy place. Indeed, the only way to know the best God has for us is to make the progression through the outer court and holy place into the most holy place. These are all symbols of the places our lives can go as we approach God according to His plan.

> *The tabernacle is a kind of invitation from God. It is a map of the journey we can take into His presence, which is where we will find the really good life.*

As I have said, for you and me, the tabernacle is like a map. When Jesus died and rose from the dead, He made a way *for all of us* into the most holy place. Instead of having to offer ritual sacrifices to reach God, we now can trust that Jesus has made the sacrifice on our behalf. Entering the presence of the glory of God in the tabernacle is available for every believer.

The tabernacle is a kind of invitation from God. It is a map of the journey we can take into His presence, which is where we will find the good life. He will not deny you, nor will He be hesitant with you, if you approach Him on His terms. We still have to approach Him according to His protocol, not according to our whims, and He is waiting to receive us when we do.

God's Opinion: Why the Altar Is Step One

When we enter the tabernacle, the first item we see is the bronze altar. This is the place of sacrifice, where blood offerings were given for the sins of the people. In order to make atonement for their wrongdoings, the Israelites would offer to God the blood of their livestock, for the blood of the animals was required by God for their sins.

Words like *sin* and *blood* (in the context of ritual sacrifice) tend to offend our modern minds. What do they mean? Why do we have to focus on these ancient concepts? This is sometimes uncomfortable, but sin and blood are foundational for understanding our relationship to God.

Sin is missing God's plan for your life. Everyone who has ever lived finds himself in this position, because no one lives God's best plan for them all the time. Actually, no one comes close at all until they learn to submit to God's Spirit.

How bad is sin? How much of a problem is it? Apart from God's mercy, sin is nothing short of devastating. God abhors sin, because He wants the best for people. Everyone who sins receives the consequences of their mistakes and punishment from God for disobedience. The altar reminds us that we need to do something about our sins so God will curtail negative natural consequences and forgive us for our disobedience.

Oh, boy, you may be thinking. *Here comes the fire and brimstone.* Well, maybe so! I'm smiling as I write this, because I think it is essential for us to accept the facts of life and learn to respond to them. We have to understand our situation in order to know what to do about it. Some people don't want to talk about the full extent of their wrongdoing, but whether they can bring themselves to face it or not, they will eventually have to deal with it. And it would be best for them and everyone around them to go ahead and face it sooner rather than later.

A television is turned on near me right now, and the news is reporting about all the people who refused to leave New Orleans before Hurricane Katrina even after a mandatory evacuation was ordered. As a result, many of them lost their lives. I understand that many people had good excuses for not evacuating, but in the end, it would have been best for them to respond to the demands to evacuate. Some may have been unable to leave, but many people simply did not take the warning seriously enough, and they paid dearly for it.

Hurricane Katrina is not an isolated case. Every day we hear about kids being unnecessarily killed in car accidents or people experimenting with dangerous drugs—all in the face of loud and clear warnings to the contrary. People who refuse to let facts speak to them suffer serious consequences.

When the apostle Paul wrote a letter to the church in Rome, he explained these same ideas.

> The wrath of God is being revealed from heaven
> against all the godlessness and wickedness of men
> who suppress the truth by their wickedness, since
> what may be known about God is plain to them,
> because God has made it plain to them.
> —Romans 1:18–19

In another letter, he outlined some specific things that incur God's wrath.

> Put to death, therefore, whatever belongs to your
> earthly nature: sexual immorality, impurity, lust,
> evil desires and greed, which is idolatry. Because
> of these, the wrath of God is coming.
> —Colossians 3:5–6

Paul taught that, deep inside, everyone intuitively knows they have sinned and that God doesn't like their sin. God wants us to live good lives, and whether we were raised in church or not, we know it.

God is real, and He has an opinion. He cares. He wants us to accept reality. He wants us to understand His feelings about our actions so that we can know how to behave. God does not want His wrath to be on anyone any more than a good dad wants his wrath to be displayed toward his children. But because good dads love their children, they do feel wrath when their children make major mistakes. Likewise, God wants to direct us toward the best possible life, and He is upset when we miss the mark.

But as we step toward the altar, we see that He has created a way to deal with our sin. Actually, He has made a way to obliterate our sin completely, as if it never happened.

Three "Altar-ing" Ideas

Justice demands that someone be punished for disobedience. We can be punished, or God can provide another to take our punishment for us. For the Israelites, God's wrath against their wrongdoing meant they had to offer a sacrifice—the blood of an animal poured upon the altar. As you can imagine, the bronze altar at the front of the tabernacle was gory, bloody, smelly, violent, and repulsive.

This gruesome mess is the first thing we see in the tabernacle. It is front and center. Why is this? Why would God want us to stop at the altar first? I can think of three reasons:

1. *God is holy.* Having the altar up front tells us that approaching God is no small matter. Something dramatic has to occur first, because He is so holy, and we are so...not. So, in the tabernacle, the priest would sacrifice animals right at the front of the altar. Because that is what it took to approach God, Jesus—who was God Himself in human form—offered Himself as a sacrifice for every person in the world. The apostle John wrote, "[Jesus] is the atoning sacrifice for our sins, and not only for ours but also for the sins of the whole world" (1 John 2:2). Jesus' blood was violently shed because of the depth of our failure to live according to the plan of our Creator, but

now that He has made the sacrifice, the way to God is wide open.

2. *Sin matters.* The Bible says, "For the wages of sin is death, but the gift of God is eternal life in Christ Jesus our Lord" (Rom. 6:23). Even if we live the best we can, we will never find the good life God has for us—or any assurance of eternal life—if we refuse to consult the One who made us. We have all done wrong, and our wrongfulness matters. We can't just wish it away. We have to deal with it before we can step further into God's good life for us. Once we do that, we can establish a trajectory for our lives that continues positively forever.

3. *God's sacrifice is more than enough.* We have done wrong, and we deserve to pay, but we don't have to. The Bible says, "This is love: not that we loved God, but that he loved us and sent his Son as an atoning sacrifice for our sins" (1 John 4:10). To love is to live—or in this case, to die—for someone else's good. God loved us so much that He did something for our good—he sent His Son as a sacrifice for us. It's done. The altar reminds us that God is holy and that we are not, but it also reminds us *that we can be* by embracing God's incredible sacrifice.

The violent, sacrificial death of Jesus is hard to think about, but it is necessary. There are some churches that will not sing or teach about the blood because it is so repugnant, but such religiosity is misguided and even arrogant. There would be no church at all without Christ's brutal death. There is no way to approach God without first embracing the sacrifice, which is why, in the tabernacle, the altar appears first.

There's Wonder-Working Power—and Protection—in the Blood

If you take a look at the illustration below, you will see that the bronze altar featured a horn on each of its corners. When an animal was sacrificed, some blood was placed on each of the four horns. Why?

First, *power*. In the Bible, horns are often a symbol of power. By instructing priests to place blood on the horns, God was communicating that the sacrifice has real, transformative power. Ritual sacrifice is not just a ceremony or an empty belief, but a powerful reality that shapes our lives. The Bible says:

> For the message of the cross is foolishness to those
> who are perishing, but to us who are being saved
> it is the power of God.   —1 Corinthians 1:18

To modern ears, the idea of blood being required sounds harsh. But it gets us closer to the messy, ugly, dirty reality of our

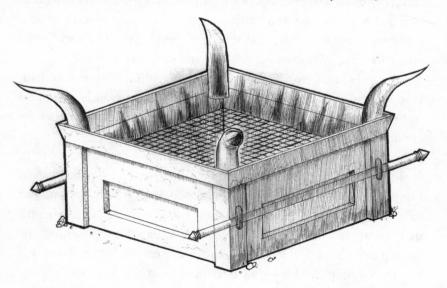

The Bronze Altar / Sacrifice and Forgiveness

lives before God, and it gives us real power to overcome sin and death.

Second, *protection*. Horns also stand for protection in the Bible, and the blood on the altar horns says that the sacrifice provides protection. Inside the tabernacle, we are protected from our own wrongdoing, and we are protected from the wrath of God. God wants to pour His blessings upon us. He wants our lives to be better. The blood of Jesus protects us from our past mistakes, and going forward, it protects us from the work of darkness against us.

The Double Whammy

Too many of us live without God's blessing in our lives. In fact, too many are living with the wrath of God working against them.

When we live according to our own plan, we sin. When we sin and do not appropriate the forgiveness of God in Christ, we receive the consequences of our thoughts, words, and actions. Our lives are often dominated by the negative consequences of wrong thinking, wrong words, and wrong actions. There is a snowball effect to this—our lives get further and further off track.

I'll say it another way. When we live according to our own plan, God's blessing is not on our lives; in fact, His wrath is on us. So not only are we living without the blessing of God, but also we are actually living a life that is fighting against God.

In my work, I see people living like this all the time, fighting against God, His plan, His purposes, His love, His Word, and His blessing. Sometimes they try to ignore God's wrath by claiming that there is no God and that their difficult lives are the result of natural processes. They often hate those who do enjoy the blessing of God. Why? Because they disagree with them? No, it's not that simple. Perhaps they hate people who enjoy God's blessing because they intuitively know that they are not enjoying that blessing. Deep down, they may recognize the truth, but rather than submitting to God's love for them, they fight. Like a rebellious teenager who goes his own way when his parents' love could offer him great relief, people like this lose the blessing God wants to give them, and it makes their lives much harder.

Still others are religious. They will not submit to God's plan for them, but they love being spiritual. They submit to rules and regulations given to them by a religious institution or a prophet they like, or maybe they make up their own spirituality. Very often these people are sincere, but sincerity doesn't matter if we are wrong.

> *When we live according to our own plan, God's blessing is not on our lives; in fact, His wrath is on us.*

Living apart from God is a double whammy. If we don't comply with God's plan, we both (1) receive the natural, negative consequences of our own errors, and (2) live under the wrath of God.

Why live like that? It makes life way too tough.

None of us need to live a life we were not designed to live, and none of us need to be separated from God. Instead, we can believe the fact that the blood of Jesus was shed for us and that God accepts His sacrifice on our behalf. This will change the direction of our lives, which will usher us toward the next place in the tabernacle—the basin.

CHAPTER FOUR

The Good Drink: Dipping Into the Good Life

The furniture in the tabernacle is an overview of how God wants us to approach Him. How do we get to know God? How do we grow deeper and deeper and *succeed* in our lives? The tabernacle layout shows us how.

Pursuing the good life is not always linear. Having explained the point of the altar in the previous chapter, I'm going to explain the significance of the basin in this chapter. But please do not begin to think that once we have passed the altar and gone on to the basin, we will never have to return to the altar again. I don't want us to get stuck in the outer court, but neither do I want us to believe that we can leave it fully behind.

Spiritual growth is about a life trajectory—moving steadily in a particular direction day after day. The general tug of your life. Trends. Tendencies. Habits. Your goal is to be the kind of person who spends more time in the holy place than in the outer court. Even though you will struggle with some sins from time to time, as you grow in maturity and strength, those struggles can become easier, shorter, and less distracting.

We have discussed the altar. Now we turn to the basin. In sum, these two items indicate what we, as New Testament believers, should experience in order to prepare us to enter the holy place, which in turn gives us an opportunity to enter the most holy place.

Absolute fullness of life is possible when we experience God as symbolized by the most holy place, but that does not mean we cannot experience something very powerful prior to the holy place. I believe that most people, including most Christians, never enter the most holy place—the holy of holies—during their lives on Earth. Actually, most never even enter the holy place at all, much less the most holy place. Most Christians stay in the outer court, leaving them short of the fullness they could be enjoying.

Why is this so? Ironically, it is partly because the outer court offers so much. There, we receive the benefits of Jesus' sacrifice from the altar and the benefits of the water of life from the basin. No question—in contrast to being completely out of fellowship with God, the outer court is incredibly satisfying.

But the court is not meant to be a final destination. It is a passage. It prepares us for a better place.

More on that later. For now, we will walk deeper into the heart of the outer court and approach the bronze basin.

Benefits of the Basin

Take a look at the bronze basin illustration on the facing page. The bronze basin was a beautiful bowl filled with water. The priests would stop at it to wash their hands and feet on the way to the holy place. In the same way, in order for us to go from the outer court to the holy place, we need to apply water from the basin to our hands and our feet.

Think of the appropriateness of that image—water cleansing our *hands* and spilling over our *feet*. We need the sanctifying

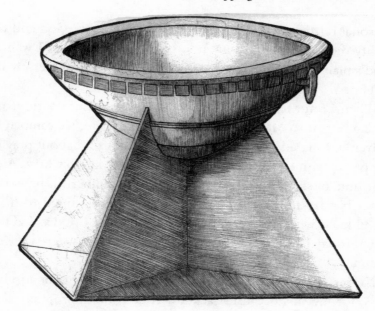

The Bronze Basin / Water Baptism and Baptism in the Holy Spirit

work of the Holy Spirit to transform our lives so that the places we go (feet) and the things we do (hands) reflect the dominance of God in our lives.

Water is an appropriate image for another reason as well. The basin represents two "water-ful" experiences that every Christian believer should have: water baptism and baptism in the Holy Spirit.

Basin basics 1: water baptism

I have had two water baptism experiences in my life. When I was a baby, my parents had me baptized in the Presbyterian church. But throughout my childhood and increasingly into my teenage years, my life was not glorifying to God. Then, when I was sixteen, our local church, Yorktown Baptist, took a vanload of youth to a conference in Dallas, Texas, called Explo '72. On Tuesday night, Bill Bright of Campus Crusade for Christ explained the fact that Jesus died on the cross for my sins, opening the door for a personal relationship with God. That night, before God and the eighty thousand students in attendance, I decided that I wanted God's plan for my life and that I was willing to surrender my life to Him.

When I returned home from the conference, our youth group took a retreat to Metamora, Indiana. While there, we camped by a river and shared our experiences in Dallas. I told about praying the prayer with Dr. Bright and committing my life to Christ. After that time of sharing, I asked my pastor, Jon Gilbert, if he would water baptize me. He wanted to do it, but he wanted to make sure I knew what I was doing. After a discussion, we decided that the next day I could be water baptized in the river where we were camping.

Notice the trajectory—I experienced atonement, or forgiveness, for my sins because I acknowledged and appropriated the blood sacrifice Jesus made for me. Then, I wanted to be baptized as a symbol of that atonement. Without even knowing it, I was progressing through the tabernacle's outer court, first passing the bronze altar, then going on to the bronze basin.

Jesus stressed water baptism when He commissioned His disciples to baptize all those who embraced their message. In a famous moment near the end of His ministry, Jesus told His disciples:

> Therefore go and make disciples of all nations,
> baptizing them in the name of the Father and of
> the Son and of the Holy Spirit, and teaching them
> to obey everything I have commanded you. And
> surely I am with you always, to the very end of
> the age.   —Matthew 28:19–20

If you have been a Christian long, no doubt you have heard or read this verse innumerable times. But even if so, notice how closely it aligns with our discussion of the tabernacle.

- He talks about becoming disciples, which requires the work of the blood in a person's life (bronze altar).

- He speaks about water baptism and obedience (bronze basin).

- Then, to give us confidence, He assures us of His presence (holy place, which you will learn about later).

Water baptism is not just a ritual, and the basin is not just a piece of furniture. Water baptism is our public declaration that our self-directed lives have been buried with Christ and that our lives are now dominated by Him. It's a place of power, as is the altar. No doubt, baptism is an important part of the spiritual walk for every person who wants to find God's plan for his or her life. Water baptism is a physical demonstration of the spiritual transformation that happens in our lives because of Christ. It communicates, both to God and to our community of fellow believers, that we want to die to our old way of life and take on the life that Christ has for us. All that can happen at the basin.

Basin basics 2: Holy Spirit baptism

The water in the bronze basin is also representative of the Holy Spirit, who is God's living water flowing through our lives. When Jesus spoke about the role of the Holy Spirit in our lives, He would often refer to the Holy Spirit as living water.

Once, Jesus was having a conversation with a woman at a well. In His illustrative way of teaching, Jesus asked her for a drink, then challenged her to think about the significance of water.

> Jesus answered her, "If you knew the gift of God and who it is that asks you for a drink, you would have asked him and he would have given you living water....Everyone who drinks this water will be thirsty again, but whoever drinks the water I

> give him will never thirst. Indeed, the water I give
> him will become in him a spring of water welling
> up to eternal life."
>
> —John 4:10, 13–14

This was early in His ministry, but already Jesus was alluding to the Holy Spirit, who is God's continual, comforting, and convicting presence in our lives.

In John 7:38, Jesus highlights the way the Holy Spirit would flow through the lives of believers:

> Whoever believes in me, as the Scripture has
> said, streams of living water will flow from within
> him.

The next verse makes it clear:

> By this he meant the Spirit, whom those who
> believed in him were later to receive. Up to that
> time the Spirit had not been given, since Jesus had
> not yet been glorified.

So, Jesus was clearly concerned that we know about the living water of His Spirit. Without living water, we thirst. We all need to be baptized in the Holy Spirit. That's why, after Jesus had risen from the dead, He told His disciples:

> Do not leave Jerusalem, but wait for the gift my
> Father promised, which you have heard me speak
> about. For John baptized with water, but in a few
> days you will be baptized with the Holy Spirit.
>
> —Acts 1:4–5

He commanded them to wait—He did not want them to try to rush forward without being baptized in the Holy Spirit. The altar (Jesus' sacrifice) and the first experience of the basin (water baptism) were wonderful, life-transforming experiences. But God had more for them. They needed to be baptized in God's Spirit as well.

The Holy Spirit Is Not Optional!

Although the bronze basin captures two defining moments in the journey of a believer—water baptism and Holy Spirit baptism—some Christian groups discourage people from being baptized with the Holy Spirit. Many encourage water baptism but are critical of Spirit baptism. But there is nothing in the Scriptures or in Christian history that would indicate that the Holy Spirit does not work today just as He did in the early church. There is nothing to indicate we should take the biblical passages about baptism in the Holy Spirit less seriously than we take baptism in water.

The Holy Spirit is not an option.

There are so many reasons to be baptized in the Holy Spirit. One is that the power of the Spirit helps us embrace the promise of the basin to help us know where we are going (our feet) and what we are doing (our hands). Indeed, Jesus emphasized that an experience with the Holy Spirit would transform our lives in such a dramatic way that we would become witnesses to the reality of the resurrection

> *To accept that being born again and water baptized is everything Christ offers us is like a child wanting their parents to stop providing for them immediately after birth.*

of Christ (Acts 1:8). In other words, with the Holy Spirit flowing through us, we increasingly become like Christ—so much so that people see the truth of Christ's resurrection by looking at us.

Actually, I am sympathetic to people's resistance to Holy Spirit baptism. I understand why people want to focus on Jesus' sacrifice and water baptism without getting into controversial conversations about the Holy Spirit. But if we want to enter the holy place, I don't think we have an option.

To accept that being born again and water baptized is every-thing Christ offers us is like a child wanting his parents to stop providing for him immediately after birth. When a child is born, it is a wonderful miracle that should be remembered as a basis for life, but it is also just the beginning of forming a baby into a responsible man or woman.

It is the same with spiritual growth. The redemption provided on the cross makes a way for us to receive all that God wants to work through us—which He delivers to us through His Holy Spirit. It is the Spirit of God who actually indwells us to transform us, teach us, convict us, and comfort us. It is through the gifts and fruit of the Holy Spirit that the benefits of Calvary become evident in us. It is by the Holy Spirit that we are able to enjoy the full life Christ offers. So we would be foolish to limit or deny anything the Holy Spirit wants to do in our lives.

Let me describe my own experience of the baptism in the Holy Spirit so you can have some context. If you have not had much exposure to Christian groups that call themselves "charismatic" (because they emphasize the "charismatic" gifts described in 1 Corinthians, such as tongues and prophecy), you might have some wrong ideas about baptism in the Holy Spirit. Actually, you might have even more wrong ideas if you *are* from a charis-matic background! I can relate to those who hesitate to embrace the baptism in the Holy Spirit because it is often associated with odd behavior, or at least behavior that seems odd at first glance. During my first few years as a Christian, I had a lively faith and an active prayer life, but I thought my friends who believed in the baptism in the Holy Spirit were off base. But I was wrong—they were just enjoying the benefits of the basin.

You see, our approach to God begins at the altar, where we acknowledge our sinfulness, repent, ask for forgiveness, and trust the blood of Christ to cleanse us. This experience is possible because the Holy Spirit draws us to Christ, and in this experience, we receive the Holy Spirit. The Holy Spirit indwells all believers. But all believers can also be baptized in the Holy Spirit.

At the basin, we experience baptism, which means "to dip or to immerse." The basin reminds us to be dipped or immersed in water, and to be dipped or immersed in the Holy Spirit.

I used to believe that all believers were automatically baptized in the Holy Spirit when they became Christians. So when I was baptized in the Spirit, it came as a shock. I had a friend who really wanted it to happen, and I agreed to pray with him one night—but I fully expected that when the night was over, he would see that he did not need anything else as a believer. Instead, as he and I prayed that night, I was the first one who experienced a deep touch of God's Spirit and began speaking in tongues! It was nothing I had to force—a prayer language just came from me like the "streams of living water" Jesus promised to His disciples. Since that day, I have enjoyed all the gifts of the Spirit from time to time, including tongues, interpretation, prophecy, and more. The baptism in the Holy Spirit opened me up to the fullest expression of the incredible benefits of trusting my life into God's care.

I have no doubt that there are people who are baptized in the Holy Spirit without a manifestation of tongues or one of the other gifts. Some teachers believe that the gift of tongues is always associated with the baptism in the Holy Spirit, but I believe it is just one of the signs of baptism. Instead, what characterize the life of a believer who has appropriated both benefits of the basin are greater faith, increased trust, easier love, and true innocence. Being immersed in the Holy Spirit gives us greater access to all the gifts of the Spirit, but it also helps us stay in the flow of God's love day in and day out.

I'll talk about these issues more later in the book. For now, before this chapter ends, I want to explore some more of the interesting water symbolism I am reminded of by the bronze basin.

The Waterworks of the Bible

The water in the basin is, first and foremost, a symbol of water and Holy Spirit baptism, but it can also serve as a reminder of (if you will) other exciting biblical waterworks. Some of the following images are strange to consider in this way, but I find them useful for understanding the many dimensions of Christ's offer of living water.

For example, in Matthew 8, Jesus casts some demons from a man into a herd of pigs, and the pigs rush into a lake and drown. The Bible says:

> He said to them [the demons], "Go!" So they came out and went into the pigs, and the whole herd rushed down the steep bank into the lake and died in the water. —Matthew 8:32

Do you see it? Water engulfed the demonic herd, just as the living water of God drowns the pigs in our lives.

I know, I know. This application is a stretch, but I think the point is true. The living water of God, the Holy Spirit, causes the pigs in our lives to die. With the altar and basin, the darkest portions of our lives never need to be victorious again. They are drowned in God's power.

Very often, even people who love what Christ did for them on the cross are embarrassed to let the water of God wash their lives.

Matthew 14 tells the famous story of Jesus and Peter walking on the water. From their boat, the disciples see Jesus walking toward them. Peter, in an act of real faith, steps out of the boat and joins Jesus on the water. But after a few steps, Peter begins to feel the rush of strong wind on the water, and his faith falters. He doesn't trust that the water will hold him up and that Jesus will protect him, and he begins to sink.

If water equals Spirit symbolically, then one of the lessons of this passage is that Jesus wants us to rely on the Spirit of God to sustain us, to keep us afloat. When Peter took his eyes off of Jesus and began to worry about his surroundings (i.e., the dangerous rush of wind), he began to fall. Note, though, that Peter cried out to Jesus, and Jesus helped him walk across the water back to the boat. If we keep our eyes on Jesus, the Spirit will sustain us.

One more water extrapolation from a famous Gospel story: Jesus washing the feet of His disciples (John 13:1–17). Jesus was humbling Himself before His friends, and Peter wanted no part of it. "No," said Peter in verse 8, "you shall never wash my feet." But Jesus rebukes him: "Unless I wash you, you have no part with me."

The point? That we have to accept the work of God on His terms. Oddly enough, Peter was being proud; it was embarrassing to see his Master kneel down. Maybe he didn't want a God who would humble Himself. But Peter had to learn to receive God on God's terms. Very often, even people who love what Christ did for them on the cross are embarrassed to let the water of God wash their lives. Arrogance, pride, and religious high-mindedness keep people from thirsting for the water that will permanently quench their thirst: drinking deep of the Holy Spirit of God.

Maybe these basin extrapolations aren't a stretch at all. The more I think about it, the more I think stopping at the basin should cause us to consider all the ways water works in the New Testament. These reflections drive us deeper and deeper into God's Word, which will help us as we go deeper into the tabernacle.

Outer Court Christianity

OK, so you have entered the tabernacle. You have believed in Jesus, received the benefits of His sacrifice, and therefore passed by the altar. You have been baptized with water and with the Holy Spirit and received the benefits available at the basin. That is wonderful, and you will never be the same.

But you have to understand that you are still in the outer court.

Many of us could stop here. And based on much of the teaching in the church, many do stop here, thinking there is nowhere else to go. Many Christians think the complete package God offers the church is a personal born-again experience in Christ, water baptism, and the filling of the Holy Spirit. That package is a wonderful, life-altering gift. Our lives have already been dramatically transformed if we have gotten this far.

But according to the symbolism of the tabernacle, there is much more.

Many Christians think the complete package God offers the church is a personal born-again experience in Christ, water baptism, and the filling of the Holy Spirit.

Want to discover it? We have been prepared in the outer court. Let's proceed to enter the holy place. Let's move from believing to becoming more like Him.

But before we do this, we need to have a family meeting. We need to get some things out in the open so we can be sure that we will find God's perfect plan for our lives—that we will really live the *best* good life. Let's have a chat. Read on.

CHAPTER FIVE

The Good Identity Shift: How God Makes You More Like Him

The truths from the tabernacle change you from the inside out. Embrace the change—let it really take root—and you will begin to live the good life.

This chapter is about that change. As we go deeper into the tabernacle, God does a miracle in us—He makes us more and more like Christ. An identity shift occurs, and we begin to identify with the mind, heart, and Spirit of Jesus. We take on His character and become an image of Him. We reflect Him.

It sounds like a miracle, doesn't it? That we could be the way we are—selfish, stressed, greedy...all in all, sinful—and change into someone resembling the greatest person who ever lived? That we could really be like Christ?

It is a miracle, and God has made it possible. It happens in people all the time, and it can happen to you as you walk further into the tabernacle.

Spiritual Accumulation:
Taking the Altar and the Basin With You

As we go forward, I want to note something that will help you to understand what is happening to you as you grow in the good life. As you progress toward the holy place and the holy of holies, it is important to remember that you are taking every experience of the tabernacle with you. The altar and the basin are not one-time events to which you never return; they are firm realities that are added to your life. They become a part of who you are.

Think of it this way: Life accumulates. Experiences add up. Our identities grow, shift, and adapt. We are not just who we are today; we are an accumulation of who we have been and what we have learned at every step along the way.

I'm forty-nine years old, but I can still remember what it felt like to be six-year-old Teddy Haggard. At times I can still identify with the little guy who liked to climb rocks, ride bicycles, go swimming, and splash everyone sunbathing beside the pool. He is a part of who I am.

From time to time, I can even identify with the seventeen-year-old in me. At that age, I loved God and church, and I also loved grabbing my friends and going to see a fast-paced action movie. I still remember what it felt like to be strong and outgoing, but also what it felt like to have an underlying insecurity and to need the approval of others. At seventeen, I was a risk-taker. I was also a little mischievous—I enjoyed comprehending things that other people hadn't considered and acting like those things were obvious. That's still a part of me.

When seventeen-year-old Ted runs into forty-nine-year-old Ted, it is a clash of worlds and a reminder that I have grown. I still know what it feels like to be seventeen; I liked being seventeen and still relish some of those memories and the wisdom learned from them. I carry them with me.

Being seventeen and all my other ages has contributed to who I am now. I am, in some way, still all the ages I have been.

You are the same way. You are whatever your age is today, but you are also all the ages you have been. If you don't believe me, ask your spouse if you ever act like a baby. (See?)

Life doesn't stop and start. It accumulates. When we go from being sixteen to seventeen, we don't lose our sixteen-year-old. We just add one more year of experience—and, I hope, wisdom—to who we are. I am forty-nine, so I can identify with being forty, thirty-five, and twenty-five. I don't have personal knowledge of being fifty-nine, but I will in another ten years. But even then, I will still have forty-nine-year-old Ted inside.

Society is the same way. We are more than humanity was one thousand years ago. We have been influenced by the thinkers and experiences of the past centuries. Life for humankind has improved in many respects because we have learned from the cumulative experiences of past generations.

Being a Christian works the same way. Our lives in Christ accumulate as we gather experiences and grow into transformation. And the tabernacle is a perfect picture of spiritual accumulation.

At the bronze altar, we learn about the gravity of our shortcomings, the importance of blood sacrifice, and the holiness of God.

Then we experience the bronze basin, where we enjoy water and Spirit baptism. Our old nature is buried with Christ through water baptism, while the Holy Spirit works His way deeply into us as we experience cleansing power that impacts what we do with our hands and where we go with our feet.

All of this prepares us to go into the holy place.

But even as we do, we cannot forget that the altar and the basin have been added to our lives.

The tabernacle is not exclusively a linear progression, taking us from one experience to another. Instead, as we walk through the tabernacle, we continually build on experiences and grow in transformation. We don't just go from one place to the next;

we take everything with us. The different moments of our spiritual experiences come together and work with one another. They accumulate and become a part of who we are, our identity as we become more like Him.

So, let's go. Let's take it all with us and really be changed as we press into the holy place.

Plenty of Room in the Outer Court

Forgetting about the altar and basin is one error. Refusing to go further is another. The outer court is a great place to be, but it's not where we want to remain. Unfortunately, many people never get any further and never really enter into the best life.

Let me let you in on a Haggardism. Don't turn this next idea into doctrine, and don't make this discussion any more than it is. But think with me for a minute.

The tabernacle is 150 feet deep and 75 feet wide, making it 11,250 square feet. Deep within the tabernacle is the holy place, which is 45 feet deep and 15 feet wide, giving it 675 square feet. The outer court, then, accounts for 94 percent of the square footage in the tabernacle. The holy place is the other 6 percent, with 2 percent of that reserved for the most holy place.

In other words, the outer court has lots and lots of room. So much room that we might think it is the most comfortable place to be. So much room that it is the place where most people stay. So many are in the outer court that we might neglect to go any further toward the holy place and most holy place, where confidence, connectivity, competence, and much more lie.

To my thinking, the dimensions of the tabernacle are a kind of warning. God might be saying to us, "I have made plenty of room in the outer court because most people will stay there. But you can come in further. I have provided the way, and I want you to come in."

The inner places of the tabernacle are special. Only a few choose to enter. Based on the dimensions of the tabernacle, we might say that 94 percent of believers in Jesus remain in the outer court, where they receive forgiveness of sins (altar) in addition to water baptism and the ministry of the Holy Spirit (basin). Sadly, some people never leave the altar—never enjoy water and Spirit baptism. Others might receive half of the benefits of the basin, but never embrace the other half. Saddest of all, only 6 percent go deeper, and of that 6 percent, only 2 percent enter the most holy place.

Remember, this is just an extrapolation. The square footage of the tabernacle might not be an indicator for New Testament Christians, and then again, it might. But here is the point: most believers appropriate the benefits of Jesus' blood sacrifice, but not all of them obey Christ by being water baptized, and some who have been water baptized don't receive the blessing available by being baptized with the Holy Spirit.

But too often, those who enter the spiritual world of repentance (altar), self-denial (water baptism), and empowerment (Spirit baptism) don't move on. So, outer court living is continual and repeated repentance, being forgiven, putting on Christ, being empowered, failing, being sorry, asking forgiveness, wanting to operate in more gifts of the Spirit, being empowered, failing, being sorry, repenting, etc. It goes on forever.

Being a Christian can be great, but for too many people, it is a constant struggle. Outer court Christians are never as confident as they could be. They repeatedly deal with the same issues over and over again. *Have I really been forgiven?* Yes—that altar makes it so! *Have I really received the Holy Spirit? Does baptism count for anything?* Yes—the basin represents God's real cleansing and empowering Spirit. But too many people remain in a struggle with their old sin nature and the transforming power of God. Too many Christians are never able to move forward into the tabernacle and the deeper places of knowing God because they are struggling to apply the blood and the power available through baptism.

It does not have to be that way. Being a Christian can be relaxing, peaceful, and easy. It can really be *the good life*. But not if we stay in the outer court.

He Identified With Us in the Outer Court. Now Let's Identify With Him in the Holy Place!

In the outer court, we celebrate the fact that God identified with us by sending His Son as a human being. The manger scene is God identifying with our humanity. The fact that Jesus was tempted in every way emphasized that He identifies with us. He understands our needs, our desires, our weaknesses, and our pain. The outer court is all about us and the forgiveness of our sins. It's about the redemption of our lives. In the outer court, we are His project.

> *As we manifest the obedience available through Christ, we enter the holy place.*

Because of this, in the outer court we learn to appreciate that God became man. Christ identified with humankind and offered Himself as a sacrifice for our sin. When we receive grace and the ministry of the Holy Spirit, we are able to do so because He identified with us in our weakness.

Then, as we grow in Christ and His Spirit, we begin to reciprocate that offering. Christ identified with us, so now we identify with Christ, abandoning our lives fully in order to take on His identity in the world.

Put plainly: entering the holy place requires an identity shift. We have to accept, believe in, and actually receive the work of the altar and the basin, thereby becoming intrinsically different. We cannot be ourselves any longer. We are new creatures.

We are already forgiven and Spirit-filled, yes, but as we *manifest the obedience available through Him*, we enter the holy place. We believe in what Christ has done for us, yes, but as we approach the holy place, we *take on His identity*. We become like Him. We are no longer the central player in our own lives. His view overtakes ours. His perspective supersedes ours. We identify with Him now.

In the holy place, His concerns become our concerns. His desires become our assignments. His projects are our calling. His thoughts are our orders. We become priests in the service of Christ with no reservations about our own interests or needs.

In the holy place, Christ burns in every portion of our lives. He overwhelms us, consumes us, and replaces us with Himself. In the holy place, we really become *Christian*—like Christ.

God Makes Us Forgiven, Not Just Sorry

Yesterday morning I was interviewed on the radio by a self-appointed evangelical watchdog. This man's project is to examine closely every well-known pulpit in America and make sure every sermon is focused on the atoning work of Christ. His finds pastors who do not meet his measure of evangelical integrity and exposes them on his radio show.

At one point in the interview, we began to talk about sin. He mentioned that every time he prayed, which was several times a day, he repented of his sins.

"That's interesting," I said. "Which sins have you repented of today?"

"Well," he responded, "I don't think I have repented of anything specifically. When I prayed this morning, I just asked God to forgive me as I always do." He thought for a second. "But you know," he continued, "the fact that I cannot think of any specific sins just proves my point. See, I'm arrogant. I should be humble enough to know of my wrongdoings at any given time. I'm glad God is gracious enough to forgive me even when I can't think of what I have done wrong."

"So," I answered, "the main work of the Holy Spirit in your life is to highlight what you do wrong?"

"He provides conviction, yes."

"Even when you don't know what He's convicting you for?"

"That's right. We should never, ever think we have nothing to repent of."

I smiled. I agreed that Christians struggle against sin, but I didn't agree that we are hopelessly bound to it.

"Do you think God's grace could help you refrain from sinning for at least a few moments?" I asked.

He said, "Yes."

"Well then, don't you think God's grace is strong enough to do more than just cover your sinfulness, but actually to liberate you from the obligation to sin?"

I tried to point out that I was talking about genuine repentance. The difference between asking for forgiveness for sin and actually repenting of sin is that if you repent, *you no longer have an obligation to sin*. Is that not part of what we are promised in the gospel?

> *I think God does more than make us sorry. I think He makes us holy.*

Nope. It didn't fly.

For this fine brother, piety meant continual prayers of sorrow and endless requests for forgiveness for sins that couldn't be remembered and probably hadn't been committed.

What a life.

It's the life of an outer court Christian.

Don't get me wrong. I understand that we all sin. I am not saying it is easy to walk in freedom from certain sins. I just think God does more than make us *sorry*. I think He makes us *holy*. The old tent preachers in the South used to say, "The purpose of the Holy Spirit is to make in us a holy...spirit."

(As an aside, I should observe that Christians often do to others what they believe God has done in them. This particular brother believes that God's role in his life is to point out his weaknesses and expose him, which is what he does to others. My view is that God's role in my life is to liberate me and empower me to be a better man, which is what I like doing for others.)

When Jesus sat down at the right hand of God the Father, after dying for us and rising from the dead, He had completed the work necessary for our victory. We were born in Him to win, not lose. We accept that truth at the altar. But to walk in this victory, we must abandon ourselves in Him.

The apostle Paul put it this way:

> I have been crucified with Christ and I no longer live, but Christ lives in me. The life I live in the body, I live by faith in the Son of God, who loved me and gave himself for me.
> —Galatians 2:20

Paul hadn't physically been crucified, but in his identification with Christ, he was in a sense as good as dead. The old Paul had been killed and replaced with Christ. Paul's life was no longer about Paul, but rather about Christ in Paul.

In his letter to the Christians in Rome, Paul communicates this same idea. Here he writes:

> For we know that our old self was crucified with him so that the body of sin might be done away with, that we should no longer be slaves to sin.
> —Romans 6:6

Paul is saying that because we are effectively "dead," we no longer have to be slaves to our old sinful impulses. Sin is no longer dominant in us because we are dead to sin. Paul argues that we no longer have to be weak, sinful Christians thanking God that we are barely saved. He says that we are no longer randomly victimized by the temptations of this world. Instead, we can be Christlike in the world.

The Outer Court Is the Beginning, Not the End

Clearly, some Christians always stay in the outer court. That's not bad; it's just incomplete.

Outer court life offers forgiveness and the initial experiences of being filled and baptized with God's Spirit. It can be wonderful. But the outer court is also a place where we constantly repent of the sin that besets us. While there, most never fully manifest the righteousness of God in Christ. While there, most never completely identify with Him. In the outer court we work on dying but are not adequately dead. Our life in Christ may be fine, but in the outer court, it is never what it could be. It is not the best life God intends for us.

Outer court Christians constantly need to learn more and more. They seek revelation all the time, hoping that *this* prayer service or *this* Bible study or *this* prophecy is going to really change them for good. They love God, but they are not able to die to themselves and put on Christ.

Putting on Christ is what can take us from the outer court into the inner court, the deeper places of knowing God. Putting on Christ leads to the good life.

The tabernacle has been said to be a picture of heaven. When Jesus died and rose from the dead, He entered the actual most holy place in heaven. He went where He wants us to go.

In the Bible, the Book of Hebrews talks about this. It says:

> He did not enter by means of the blood of goats and calves; but he entered the Most Holy Place once for all by his own blood, having obtained eternal redemption.
>
> —Hebrews 9:12

After doing this, Jesus sat down at the right hand of Majesty. That is why Hebrews also says:

> But when this priest [Jesus] had offered for all time one sacrifice for sins, he sat down at the right hand of God. Since that time he waits for his enemies to be made his footstool, because by one sacrifice he has made perfect forever those who are being made holy.
>
> —Hebrews 10:12–14

Look closely at this. Jesus offered the sacrifice for our sins, and by this one sacrifice He has made *perfect forever those who are being made holy.*

That's us. We are being made holy.

That's how life becomes truly good when we live in the tabernacle.

What Happens When You Identify With Christ

When Paul wrote a letter to the church in Ephesus, he explained to them the great benefits of taking on Christ's identity. The letter says:

> [God] made us alive with Christ even when we were dead in transgressions—it is by grace you have been saved. And God raised us up with Christ and seated us with him in the heavenly realms in Christ Jesus.
>
> —Ephesians 2:5–6

See that? God raised us up with Christ and seated us with Him. What does this mean? It means we have spiritual authority in Christ. God has extended to us the ability to operate in Jesus' name.

When we pray "in Jesus' name," we are not just mimicking some Christian habit. We are actually praying in His stead, in His place, with His authority. We are Christ's representatives on Earth. When we embrace this truth, we can help do the work of God in the world.

When you identify with Christ, you have been crucified.

When you identify with Christ, you have been buried.

When you identify with Christ, you have been raised from the dead.

When you identify with Christ, you have ascended to the right hand of God the Father.

When you identify with Christ, you have authority.

A little earlier in Paul's same letter to the Ephesians, he wrote a bit about the authority Christ has:

> That power is like the working of his mighty strength, which he exerted in Christ when he raised him from the dead and seated him at his right hand in the heavenly realms, far above all rule and authority, power and dominion, and every title that can be given, not only in the present age but also in the one to come. And God placed all things under his feet and appointed him to be head over everything for the church, which is his body, the fullness of him who fills everything in every way.
>
> —Ephesians 1:19–23

All things under His feet. If we have His authority, then we can accomplish great things by appropriating that authority for God's work in the earth.

The world needs men and women of God who have the joy of a clear conscience with the confidence that God is working in their lives. God wants us to be about His business. He doesn't want us consumed with our own sinfulness, nor does He want us always praying about ourselves. He wants us to utilize the blood of Christ and the power of the Spirit so we can do His work.

The Bible says that we are no longer orphans, but we are actually God's children. (See John 14:18; 1 John 3:1.) Why would God say that? Because He wants us to know that we now share His nature.

In *Victory Over the Darkness: Realizing the Power of Your Identity in Christ*, Neil Anderson lists some of the benefits we have in Christ. Here's what God does for us when we put on Christ:

- He calls us His friends (John 15:15).

- He says that we are justified (Rom. 5:1).

- He says that we are one spirit with Him (1 Cor. 6:17).

- He says that we belong to Him (1 Cor. 6:19–20).

- He says that we are members of His body (1 Cor. 12:27).

- He says that we are holy people—saints (Eph. 1:1).

- He says that we have been adopted into His family (Eph.1:5).

- He says that we have direct access to God (Eph. 2:18).

- He says that we have been forgiven of all of our sins (Col. 1:14).

- He says that we are complete (Col. 2:10).*

There is no way we can read this list and the attendant scriptures and think that we are powerless slaves to sinfulness who will never enjoy the reality of Christ's work in our lives. But this isn't all. Anderson also offers a list of our new identity traits as we take on Christ's role for us:

- We are God's salt of the earth (Matt. 5:13).

- We are God's light of the world (Matt. 5:14).

- We are God's channel of life (John 15:1, 5).

- We are God's choice to demonstrate His fruit (John 15:16).

- We are God's evidence to others that He is real (Acts 1:8).

- We are God's dwelling place (1 Cor. 3:16).

- We are God's ambassadors of reconciliation (2 Cor. 5:17–21).

- We are God's co-workers (2 Cor. 6:1).

- We are God's workmanship, created for good works (Eph. 2:10).

I fear that my friend with the Christian radio show was not building on the full work of the altar and the basin, and he could not understand how significantly he could die and take on Christ. He was fixated on his own condition rather than his identification with Christ. He was, in effect, stuck in the outer court, and perhaps just at the altar.

---

*This list and the two following lists are adapted from Neil T. Anderson, *Victory Over the Darkness: Realizing the Power of Your Authority in Christ*, tenth anniversary edition (Ventura, CA: Regal Books, 2000), 38–39.

Again, the outer court is the foundation for everything we need. But it is too often perpetual victimization and restoration. It's continual pressure and appreciation and liberation. It's believing and receiving, but not becoming. It's reading, believing, and seeking the good life, but instead of manifesting the holiness that is available, guilt or failure relaunch the cycle of repentance again.

Outer court living is a lot of work. No doubt, our lives change there. But we can keep going. God wants to display His love and power through us. But if we stay in the outer court, we will never get over ourselves. Again from Neil Anderson:

- I am free from condemnation (Rom. 8:1–2).

- I am assured that all things work together for good (Rom. 8:28).

- I am free from any condemning charges against me (Rom. 8:31–34).

- I cannot be separated from the love of God (Rom. 8:35–39).

- I have been established, anointed, and sealed by God (2 Cor. 1:21–22).

- I am confident that the good work God has begun in me will be perfected (Phil. 1:6).

- I am a citizen of heaven (Phil. 3:20).

- I am hidden with Christ in God (Col. 3:3).

- I have not been given a spirit of fear but of power, love, and discipline (2 Tim. 1:7).

- I can find grace and mercy to help me in times of need (Heb. 4:16).

- I am born of God, and the evil one cannot touch me (1 John 5:18).

Hopefully by now you are convinced, motivated, and ready to move forward. But you might still be wondering one thing: how?

How do we really do it? How do we move beyond the altar and the basin and identify with Christ? How do we deny ourselves? How do we get past ourselves to the point that we are consumed with His purposes rather than our own issues? How do we move toward pursuing the good life of real confidence, real connection with others, and more?

There is an answer, and it is remarkably simple: manifested obedience. We will discuss it next.

CHAPTER SIX

The Good Choice:
Why It's Up to You

I can't do it. I just can't do it. I am supposed to write a chapter on the incredible exhilaration that comes into our lives as we learn to manifest the obedience Christ offers. I want to encourage you and help you see that if you appropriate His obedience and walk in it, you will enter the holy place and experience the life that is truly life—the good life.

This chapter is supposed to be positive. This chapter is where everything falls into place. This is where I will explain the two options we should have at this point—to either remain in the outer court enjoying the altar (forgiveness) and the basin (baptism), or to joyfully walk into the holy place. This chapter is supposed to be about victory, the end of frustration, and a life of power, delight, and purpose.

Wouldn't that be a great chapter?

But I've been staring at my computer screen all morning. I cannot bring myself to write a single word.

Here's what is stopping me—I want to write about those two options, but I can't, because I know there is a third. We can stay in the outer court, as most people do. Or we can manifest His obedience and enter the holy place. But there is a third option for us. And sadly, many people take it.

We can just walk away.

It's a terrible thought, but the fact is that some people are in the outer court, but they become discouraged and…go home. They leave. They don't find the secret to manifesting His obedience in their daily lives, and they get tired of the cycle of sin, repentance, forgiveness, sin, repentance, forgiveness, so they just stop. They get tired and sometimes angry or judgmental, and they leave.

Theologians have been conflicted about this option for centuries, and with good reason. Many scriptures in the Bible give us assurance of eternal life—saying that we are sealed until the day of redemption and that nothing can separate us from the love of God. Theologians rightly emphasize these scriptures, and I too believe these promises are true.

But the theologians who stake their claims on these promises sometimes don't balance their interpretation, and they exclude other portions of the Bible that say believers can, in effect, become nonbelievers, or can at least choose to reject God's grace. It is a terrible thought, and I hate to consider it in a book on the good life, but I cannot avoid it.

All of my Christian life, the last thirty-three years, I have watched people leave the outer court, not to go into the holy place, but to go home. Some leave the faith entirely. How is that possible? Had they not adequately repented? Had they not been water baptized? Had they not been baptized with the Holy Spirit? It's true, many had not, but I don't think it can explain all of them.

Theologians who claim that all believers are eternally secure usually say of such people that they must have never really visited the altar (repented and accepted Jesus' sacrifice) or experienced the basin (been water and Spirit baptized). They often say people who walk away from the faith were never really Christians in the first place.

No doubt, this is true, but I don't believe it's true for everyone. I am too old to keep saying that everyone who leaves the faith must not have ever known Christ. I have seen and experienced too much. I have read too much Bible to gloss over the hard realities with theological constructions that explain away contrary scriptures. I believe that people can be authentically saved, experience water baptism, taste the power of the Holy Spirit, and still go back to the world and miss God's plan for their lives...the good life.

So you can see why I have had trouble writing this morning. It would be deceptive for me to encourage you to move forward by manifesting His obedience in you, giving you the impression that the only choices you have at this point are to stay in the outer court or go into the holy place.

The fact is, you have to decide. Are you going to stay in the outer court? Are you going to go into the holy place? Or are you going to leave?

Heaven Seems Too Far Away

We all know that every one of us will deal with sin. Even though sin does not need to rule over us as Christians, we will continue to struggle with sin while here on Earth, and we will, in fact, sin from time to time.

But outer court Christians struggle more than others. They have not identified with Christ in such a way that righteousness is manifested in their lives. In the outer court, sin is the norm and holiness is the exception. In the holy place, holiness is the norm and sin is the exception. In the outer court, every temptation is a major struggle. Sometimes the struggle dominates their entire

Christian experiences. Sometimes their life is a preponderance of guilt and condemnation.

And sometimes, they get tired of the grind, and they decide to leave. They walk away from the tabernacle of God. They either become passive and do other things, or they become hostile. Either way, they leave the Christian faith behind. They stop pursuing the good life of Jesus.

I get it. I don't blame them. I understand why they take off. The cycle of sin, conviction, repentance, and sin is exhausting. It is easy to think the perpetual guilt isn't worth it. Heaven seems too far away.

- We can go into the holy place, with unquestionable evidence that we have been sealed until the day of redemption.

- Or we can stay in the outer court and keep trying to work it out.

- Or we can walk away entirely.

Before we talk about how obedience takes us into the holy place, I feel I must, with a heavy heart, spend this chapter discussing the option to walk away from God.

What the Bible Says

Years ago I read some verses that sobered me and forced me to press into the holy place.

I knew that my life rested on the altar and basin in the outer court, but I felt stuck there. One set of theologians told me that there was nothing to the Christian life past the altar and water baptism. I appreciated forgiveness and redemption, and I embraced self-denial in being buried with Christ in baptism.

Then when I was baptized with the Holy Spirit I appreciated the additional power and life so much. I was elated. But this left me somewhat trapped until I learned that these provisions and experiences were the basis for, the foundation for, the fundamental preparations for...a great life. They were not the end, but the beginning.

But others were not telling me that. Instead, I felt stuck in frustration and guilt. And I had, in fact, contemplated leaving. I wanted to go deeper in Christ. I didn't want to stay in the same place, nor did I want to leave.

As I was reading Hebrews that day, I came to the tenth chapter, verses 26–31:

> If we deliberately keep on sinning after we have received the knowledge of the truth, no sacrifice for sins is left, but only a fearful expectation of judgment and of raging fire that will consume the enemies of God. Anyone who rejected the law of Moses died without mercy on the testimony of two or three witnesses. How much more severely do you think a man deserves to be punished who has trampled the Son of God under foot, who has treated as an unholy thing the blood of the covenant that sanctified him, and who has insulted the Spirit of grace? For we know him who said, "It is mine to avenge; I will repay." And again, "The Lord will judge his people." It is a dreadful thing to fall into the hands of the living God.

I know we hope this does not apply to anyone who knows the Lord, but the context does not indicate that. The immediate meaning of these verses makes it clear enough that the writer had believers in mind, don't you think? Furthermore, the chapters prior to these verses are 100 percent directed at those who believe, and the chapters following these verses are clearly for believers as well.

This is a warning, and it is clear whom the warning is for. It is for believers. It is for us.

What do you think it means to "treat as an unholy thing the blood of the covenant that sanctified him" and to "insult the Spirit of grace"? Could that apply to believers who sin, repent with words, sin, repent with words, sin, repent with words, sin, repent with words, over and over again until they come to a place of frustration where they say, "I'm out of here! I still like my sin, and I'm not repenting anymore!"?

I don't think God ever resists anyone who repents. Actually, I don't believe any of us can repent unless God's Spirit woos us. (See John 6:44.) But when we repent, He will never leave us or forsake us.

But for Christians whose lives do not progress in holiness, it is natural to consider giving up. And, sadly, some do. They stop repenting and surrender to their lot.

Some do it in a moment, but others slowly slip away. They may still believe in God and pray from time to time and read their Bibles, but they are not constant. They have stopped pursuing the life found only in God. Many do not want to meet with other believers (as warned about in Hebrews 10:25) and try to form a spiritual life on their own. Why? Maybe because there is less guilt. Fewer obligations. Fewer exhortations to improve.

Some theologians would say that once a person is born again, their eternal destiny is secure no matter what happens from that day forward. But I think it would be unwise to trust those theologians and risk so much. If these types of decisions could not impact our eternities, the Bible would not warn us so directly in Hebrews 3:12:

> See to it, brothers, that none of you has a sinful, unbelieving heart that turns away from the living God.

Clearly, this is to "brothers," or fellow believers, and is an exhortation against turning away.

This is tough stuff. Instead of pounding it home, I want to give you a chance to think through it for yourself.

I have communicated the main idea, and I want to give you a chance to meditate on it. For most of the rest of this chapter, I am going to list some scriptures for you to read. Rather than excerpting some scripture, elaborating on it, excerpting some more, and so on, I want to let these verses speak for themselves. After a selection of pertinent scriptures, I will sum up some ideas at the end.

> *In order to move forward toward the good life in God, we have to grasp the reality of all our options as Christians. Even the darkest option.*

Don't flip forward. I know people often skip over sections like this in Christian living books, but I'm asking you to study these verses closely. Mark them in your own Bible, and read around these passages for further context.

My goal here is not to discourage you but to warn you, and then to encourage you to move your life in the right direction—through the outer court and into the holy place. So be encouraged. Move your life in the right direction. In order to move forward toward the good life in God, we have to grasp the reality of all our options as Christians. Even the darkest option.

Let's read these Bible verses. And let's determine never to leave the tabernacle, but to remain in it forever and strive to fulfill God's purpose for our lives.

* * * * *

Woe to you, Korazin! Woe to you, Bethsaida! If the miracles that were performed in you had been performed in Tyre and Sidon, they would have repented long ago in sackcloth and ashes. But I tell you, it will be more bearable for Tyre and Sidon on the day of judgment than for you. And you, Capernaum, will you be lifted up to the skies? No, you will go down to the depths. If the miracles that were performed in you had been performed in Sodom, it would have remained to this day.

—Matthew 11:21–23

Watch out that no one deceives you. For many will come in my name, claiming, "I am the Christ," and will deceive many.

—Matthew 24:4–5

And many false prophets will appear and deceive many people. Because of the increase of wickedness, the love of most will grow cold, but he who stands firm to the end will be saved.

—Matthew 24:11–13

I [Jesus] am the true vine, and my Father is the gardener. He cuts off every branch in me that bears no fruit, while every branch that does bear fruit he prunes so that it will be even more fruitful. You are already clean because of the word I have spoken to you. Remain in me, and I will remain in you. No branch can bear fruit by itself; it must remain in the vine. Neither can you bear fruit unless you remain in me. I am the vine; you are the branches. If a man remains in me and I in him, he will bear much fruit; apart from me you can do nothing. If anyone does not remain in me, he is like a branch that is thrown away and withers; such branches are picked up, thrown into the fire and burned.

—John 15:1–6

They preached the good news in that city and won a large number of disciples. Then they returned to Lystra, Iconium and Antioch, strengthening the disciples and encouraging them to remain true to the faith. "We must go through many hardships to enter the kingdom of God," they said.

—Acts 14:21–22

Now, brothers, I want to remind you of the gospel I preached to you, which you received and on which you have taken your stand. By this gospel you are saved, if you hold firmly to the word I preached to you. Otherwise, you have believed in vain.

—1 Corinthians 15:1–2

Once you were alienated from God and were enemies in your minds because of your evil behavior. But now he has reconciled you by Christ's physical body through death to present you holy in his sight, without blemish and free from accusation— if you continue in your faith, established and firm, not moved from the hope held out in the gospel. This is the gospel that you heard and that has been proclaimed to every creature under heaven, and of which I, Paul, have become a servant.

—Colossians 1:21–23

The Spirit clearly says that in later times some will abandon the faith and follow deceiving spirits and

things taught by demons....Watch your life and
doctrine closely. Persevere in them, because if you
do, you will save both yourself and your hearers.
—1 Timothy 4:1, 16

For the love of money is a root of all kinds of evil.
Some people, eager for money, have wandered
from the faith and pierced themselves with many
griefs. But you, man of God, flee from all this,
and pursue righteousness, godliness, faith, love,
endurance and gentleness. Fight the good fight
of the faith. Take hold of the eternal life to which
you were called when you made your good con-
fession in the presence of many witnesses.
—1 Timothy 6:10–12

Preach the Word; be prepared in season and out of
season; correct, rebuke and encourage—with great
patience and careful instruction. For the time will
come when men will not put up with sound doctrine. Instead, to suit their own desires, they will
gather around them a great number of teachers to
say what their itching ears want to hear. They will
turn their ears away from the truth and turn aside
to myths. But you, keep your head in all situations, endure hardship, do the work of an evange-
list, discharge all the duties of your ministry.
—2 Timothy 4:2–5

We must pay more careful attention, therefore, to
what we have heard, so that we do not drift away.
For if the message spoken by angels was binding,
and every violation and disobedience received its
just punishment, how shall we escape if we ignore
such a great salvation? This salvation, which was

first announced by the Lord, was confirmed to us by those who heard him.

—Hebrews 2:1–3

But Christ is faithful as a son over God's house. And we are his house, if we hold on to our courage and the hope of which we boast. So, as the Holy Spirit says: "Today, if you hear his voice, do not harden your hearts as you did in the rebellion, during the time of testing in the desert…" See to it, brothers, that none of you has a sinful, unbelieving heart that turns away from the living God. But encourage one another daily, as long as it is called Today, so that none of you may be hardened by sin's deceitfulness. We have come to share in Christ if we hold firmly till the end the confidence we had at first.

—Hebrews 3:6–8, 12–14

It is impossible for those who have once been enlightened, who have tasted the heavenly gift, who have shared in the Holy Spirit, who have tasted the goodness of the word of God and the powers of the coming age, if they fall away, to be brought back to repentance, because to their loss they are crucifying the Son of God all over again and subjecting him to public disgrace.

—Hebrews 6:4–6

My brothers, if one of you should wander from the truth and someone should bring him back, remember this: Whoever turns a sinner from the error of his way will save him from death and cover over a multitude of sins.

—James 5:19–20

For if you possess these qualities in increasing measure, they will keep you from being ineffective and unproductive in your knowledge of our Lord Jesus Christ. But if anyone does not have them, he is nearsighted and blind, and has forgotten that he has been cleansed from his past sins. Therefore, my brothers, be all the more eager to make your calling and election sure. For if you do these things, you will never fall, and you will receive a rich welcome into the eternal kingdom of our Lord and Savior Jesus Christ.

—2 Peter 1:8–11

No one who denies the Son has the Father; whoever acknowledges the Son has the Father also. See that what you have heard from the beginning remains in you. If it does, you will also remain in the Son and in the Father. And this is what he promised us—even eternal life.

—1 John 2:23–25

* * * * *

Now What?
Choose the Good Life!

Every person who walks away from God takes a different path, but I have observed common characteristics among my friends who have drifted away, or seem to be drifting. Many of them thought they were becoming well informed, but they really just became enamored with ideas that cooled their passion for God. They judged God and His followers, and they thought of themselves more highly. Many of them remained Christians for a while, but only intellectually—they had no heart connectivity to God or the church. They were skilled at judging problems with the church but terrible at actually serving the church.

For others, as I mentioned earlier in this chapter, sin issues dominated them for so long that they eventually gave up. They stayed at the bronze altar for years, or just went back and forth between the altar and the basin without ever receiving instruction on how to enter the holy place. The Christian life became too difficult because righteousness was too hard to obtain, and they became tired. Many of them blamed the church as well, even though their most central problem was a personal sin issue.

The great tragedy of failed Christians is that they are making life harder than it has to be. Jesus said His burden was easy and His yoke was light. Paul said he didn't want his ministry to be a burden to anyone.

I have always believed that growing in Christ can be easy, but that is a hard sell among modern Christians. In writing one of my previous books, I wrote four different times how easy it was to be a Christian. Each time, the editor removed the point. I fought to put it back in, but I finally lost. The editor was so convinced that Christian living was not easy that she insisted that I not even try to present that argument. But I believe it.

> *The great tragedy of failed Christians is that they are making life harder than it has to be.*

Maybe the issue is that the outer court is hard, but the holy place is easy. In the outer court, even though you have accepted the love of Jesus and the life of the Spirit, you spend much of your time wrestling for sanctification. For those who go into the holy place, the burden of guilt is gone, the compelling tug of sin is broken, and life takes on a new dimension.

Remember, God has done everything reasonable to cause us to stay in the tabernacle. He wants us to enter the good life. The Holy Spirit wants to draw us closer, not let us slip away. He tells us how in Hebrews 10:19–25, where the author is calling the church to perseverance:

> Therefore, brothers, since we have confidence to enter the Most Holy Place by the blood of Jesus, by a new and living way opened for us through the curtain, that is, his body, and since we have a great priest over the house of God, let us draw near to God with a sincere heart in full assurance of faith, having our hearts sprinkled to cleanse us from a guilty conscience and having our bodies washed with pure water. Let us hold unswervingly to the hope we profess, for he who promised is faithful. And let us consider how we may spur one another on toward love and good deeds. Let us not give up meeting together, as some are in the habit of doing, but let us encourage one another—and all the more as you see the Day approaching.

Then in Ephesians 4:30, the Bible says:

> And do not grieve the Holy Spirit of God, with whom you were sealed for the day of redemption.

You were sealed. Trust that. Believe it. Live in it.

Now that we have covered the three options we have, let's get back to our pursuit. Let's talk about how manifesting Christ's obedience in our lives keeps us moving into the holy place.

Let's go. Let's choose to pursue the good life.

Part Three

Moving Forward in the Good Life

The holy place is a shift in focus. In the outer court, we appreciated the way Christ identified with us as humans—He became a man, took on our sins, and died in our place. Now, as we learn to take on Christ's identity, we do what He did: we die (to ourselves) and are raised (to live in Him).

CHAPTER SEVEN

Better Actions: Better Life

Y ou have experienced the outer court, and you have decided never to leave the tabernacle. Now, to go into the holy place, you have to manifest obedience. That means you experience victory over your old habits and shortcomings. Obedience to God's ways becomes your identity. I call this "manifest obedience" because this is where we let the power of righteousness overwhelm the power of sin. This is not burdensome. Instead, it is freedom—freedom to be godly, the way you really want to be, freedom to live the good life.

It is possible. It can be done. And it is the key that unlocks the door to living in the holy place...which means living the good life God has for us all.

Why is obedience the key to moving from the outer court into the holy place? Because obedience is a tangible display—an active manifestation—of the work God has done in our lives. When we obey, we show that we have taken on Christ's identity. We spend less time messing with temptations and other distractions. We are unflinchingly devoted to God.

The holy place is a shift in focus. In the outer court, we appreciated the way Christ identified with us as humans—He became a man, took on our sins, and died in our place. Now, as we learn to take on Christ's identity, we do what He did: we die (to ourselves) and are raised (to live in Him).

Another way of saying it is that as we move from the outer court toward the holy place, we go from just *believing* to actually *becoming*. Prior to entering the holy place, when we read the Bible, we believe it, but the virtue and life described in the Bible are not all automatically imparted into our core. But at this point in our journey where the grip of sin is breaking and obedience is increasingly natural, we transition into actually becoming the person the Bible says we can be. Now, we begin to embody the very characteristics of Christ, and those characteristics become obvious to everyone we know.

> *As we move from the outer court toward the holy place, we go from just* believing *to actually* becoming.

As we go into the holy place, we are no longer the central figure in our lives. God's will is front and center. We realize that God has a plan in the earth that is going to be fulfilled, and we want to be involved with that plan. As we are increasingly focused on the things that interest Him, we merge our lives into His plans and purposes for the world.

For the most part, this is what has happened in my life. I no longer believe that life is about me, my interests, or my plans. I believe that God has a grand plan for the world, and I am sovereignly synchronized with that plan. As I let the things that move His heart move mine, and as I walk in obedience and identification with Him, I become a tool, a friend, that God uses to help fulfill the plan. It's easier than outer court living.

Holy Place Prayer

One indication of holy place obedience is what happens in our prayer times. Many Christians—you know, outer court Christians—spend the majority of their prayer times focused on their own issues. It is as if they think the Lord's Prayer begins and ends with "Forgive us our sins." But in the holy place, we

**The Holy Place / Identifying With Christ
and Manifesting Obedience**

are so convinced of God's grace and we are so committed to the practice of obedient living that our prayer times can be about much more.

At New Life Church, where I serve as senior pastor, our campus includes the World Prayer Center, which is a building dedicated to this idea that prayer is about more than me and you and our daily struggles. The center coordinates the most-used Internet prayer site in the world, worldprayerteam.org. New Life Church spends time and resources on projects like this because we believe that holy place living helps us accomplish great things in prayer. We believe hearts and minds, and even cities and nations, can be transformed through the power of prayer.

The apostle John wrote:

> Dear friends, if our hearts do not condemn us, we
> have confidence before God and receive from him
> anything we ask, because we obey his commands
> and do what pleases him.   —1 John 3:21–22

In other words, our actions affect our confidence in prayer. When we live as God wants us to live, we can pray and know that God hears and answers, and so our prayers can focus on essential, urgent matters all around the world. We focus less on "Forgive us our sins" and more on "Your kingdom come, Your will be done."

This is holy place obedience—letting your will and ways die, living entirely for God, and being part of His work in the earth.

Your Story in God's Story

In the holy place, we tend to stop wrestling with our place in the body of Christ. We don't worry about it, because we figure out that it's not about us in the first place. It's about God, His church, the world, and eternity.

Remember, the story of God and His plan for His creation is a metanarrative—an over-arching, transcendent story that tells us the meaning of life. Our lives are individual micronarratives, the stories within the big story. For example, I am the subplot. I am not the main character; the body of Christ as a whole is the main character. I am included because I am a member of the body of Christ. I am a contributor to the story being fulfilled, but the story is not about me.

I am a part, not the whole. God's perfect plan for my life is my role within the whole.

Think of Susanna Wesley. You may not have heard of her, but you have probably heard of her two boys, John and Charles Wesley. Or you have heard of the denomination they founded, the Methodist Church. John and Charles changed the world through their preaching, teaching, and music ministry, but their mom helped shaped them into the men of God they were to become.

Susanna had a methodology for everything she did, whether cleaning house, preparing meals, or getting the kids to church. Many believe her approach to everyday tasks helped shape the way her two boys approached the Christian life. They too developed methodologies for conversion and discipleship, which is why the churches they founded developed the name "Method-ist." The groups that used the Wesleys' theology and methods resulted in churches that have brought life to millions and millions of people. John and Charles may have been the most significant people of their generation, but they never would have been who they became without their mother. As a result, their mother might have been the most significant person in her generation. But no one knew it. She was raising her kids...who forever impacted history. Even Susanna Wesley could not have known that. She just lived faithfully, and the seemingly small role she played in God's metanarrative helped change the world.

I'm sure that many days Susanna had no desire to clean clothes or prepare dinner. I'm sure she sometimes felt like lying in bed all day. But she was a servant, and she served. She did not understand the role she was playing in God's narrative. But because she was obedient to play her part, millions more people have experienced the life of God.

Think also of Joseph in Potiphar's house and prison (Gen. 39–41), being frustrated day in, day out. He had dreams, he had a calling, and he had a clear sense of where he wanted to be. But for many years, he just had to play a small role without understanding why. Today, we can read the whole Joseph story in one sitting, and we can draw lessons from his life. But at the time, for Joseph, it didn't make any sense. He just had to trust God.

Going into the holy place requires accepting your micronarrative. It means trusting God. It means you forfeit your life and blend into God's metanarrative for the earth.

Paul wrote:

> And we know that in all things God works for
> the good of those who love him, who have been
> called according to his purpose.   —Romans 8:28

Notice what this tells us about God's plan. All things work together for the good of those who love God (this means they are living for God's good, not their own) and have been called according to His purpose. In other words, when we have been called by God, His purpose for the world is our purpose. Our story is part of His big story. Our micronarrative comes alive within His metanarrative. Our life has context because it is a piece of His long-term, global plan.

How God's Story Shifts Your Perspective

Understanding that our lives are roles in a bigger story means we see things differently. We develop a sense of the long-term goals, of the overall trajectory of history. An old joke says a day in the

Vatican is one hundred years, and likewise, we who are part of God's metanarrative do not get overly hung up on temporary problems or situations. We see every day in terms of the long view.

The average soldier in World War II probably had a hard time appreciating his orders, but the generals knew what they were doing. Generals and presidents see the whole story. Soldiers live out the micronarrative. That's the way we fit into God's great plan—like soldiers obeying our leader, even if the course of action does not make sense from our point of view.

The Bible says:

> For he chose us in him before the creation of the world to be holy and blameless in his sight. In love he predestined us to be adopted as his sons through Jesus Christ, in accordance with his pleasure and will.
>
> —Ephesians 1:4–5

Read this thinking of your micronarrative in God's metanarrative, and you can see that:

- *God chose you in Him.* What does this mean? Some think it means that He forces people to be saved. I don't think so. I think it means that your plan and purposes for life are found in Him. Direction and eternal significance are found in Him. A Haggard paraphrase would be, "God's plan for you can only be fulfilled when you live in God."

- *God established His plan for you before the creation of the world.* You are not an accident. You are not merely the biological result of your mom and dad getting together. God has a plan for this generation that has been scheduled from the beginning of time, and you are destined to be part of that plan.

- *God plans for you to be holy and blameless in His sight.* We can fulfill God's plan, but if we live in sin, it will throw our lives off track. Our portion of the story will be incomplete. To play our part in the overall scheme of God for the earth, we need to be set apart for His work and strive to be holy.

- *God loves you so much that He wrote you into His script.* God really wants you to live in Him. He wants to use you to help Him do what He wants to do. He wants you to be His child and to accept your role in the overall story.

What Happens Inside the Holy Place

As we walk into the holy place, the first thing we recognize is that we have been *set apart as holy.* Our actions are no longer determined by what we think is best or by how we have been trained. Instead, our actions are determined by our understanding of His kingdom, His will and purposes in the earth, and the reality that we are dead to ourselves and alive in Him.

Second, we have embraced the idea that our lives are *separate from the world.* The earth is no longer our home. Our values are no longer the values of this world. We are representatives of heaven on the earth, sent here by God in order to work for His kingdom. The purpose of our lives is to let a slice of heaven operate here on the earth. Our job is to rescue people from worldly living and demonstrate that there is a kingdom other than the kingdom of this world. We do not think or act in the way citizens of this world think and act. Instead, we live with the hope of another world.

Third, our lives are *consecrated to God*. Our bodies are not for the purposes of our own pleasure; they are instruments belonging to God for His glory. Our minds, mouths, ears, hands, and feet are His tools—not ours and not the world's. Our resources, time, influence, and futures are not ours, but God's. So whatever we do, wherever we go, whatever we say, it is an act of submission to God.

And last, we dispense with the way we wrestled with sin so much in the outer court, and we are *set free from sin*. Our prayer times are no longer concerned with a search for continual forgiveness; we are sure of God's forgiveness working in us. In the outer court, sin was the norm and holiness the exception, but in the holy place, holiness is the norm and sin is the exception. In the holy place, the fact that believers have no obligation to sin is a working reality, not a distant dream. In the holy place, the fact that we are new creations in Christ is manifested in daily living, not something we just read and believe but never experience.

What does all this mean? It means that as we walk into the holy place—as we receive God's grace, become like Christ, and really begin to *live* it—we are forever changed. We are in pursuit of the good life, and nothing can hold us back.

Are We Bound to Sin?

Can freedom from sin really be had? Is natural obedience possible for all Christians? I think so. I have believed for years that the Christian life is easy, but I have faced opposition from many fine Christians. And it is easy to see why—it is tough to feel sinless when sin creeps in so easily, as it does for most of us.

But now I think I have discovered a crucial distinction: outer court living is a vicious, continual struggle, but in holy place living, the struggle is largely settled.

In the holy place, we don't just *strive for* intimate fellowship with God; we *abide in it*. We serve His kingdom because doing so gives us joy, not because we are compelled by guilt.

In the holy place, the gentle whisper of the Holy Spirit is natural; it is the norm, not the exception.

In the holy place, joy is a natural state, not a distant hope.

In the holy place, dominant sin is not the main story of our lives; it's the story of our pasts.

> *If we will love God and love others as ourselves, we will never sin.*

The apostle Peter believed in this. He wrote of those "who have been chosen according to the foreknowledge of God the Father, through the sanctifying work of the Spirit, for obedience to Jesus Christ and sprinkling by his blood" (1 Pet. 1:2). This "who" is you and me—people who have decided to follow Christ. Peter is saying that we were chosen by God from long, long ago.

And what are we chosen for? "Obedience to Jesus Christ." Obedience—a life that is true, selfless, consistent, and steady. This is not a distant dream. It is the very thing we are chosen for.

Obedience is a wonderful delight, a joyful liberation. It is not hard, and it is not difficult; it is a road of entry into the holy place.

You Can Be Obedient. Here's How.

Jesus made obedience so simple that it is tough to understand why we make it so complicated. He said:

> "Love the Lord your God with all your heart and with all your soul and with all your mind." This is the first and greatest commandment. And the

second is like it: "Love your neighbor as yourself."
All the Law and the Prophets hang on these two
commandments.

—Matthew 22:37–40

Here's what this means to me. If we will love God and love others as ourselves, we will never sin. My simple definition of love, as I mentioned earlier, is "to live for the good of another." So, if we live for the good of God and the good of others, we will not sin.

People who live for the good of God and others don't commit adultery, steal, lie, or hate. It just doesn't happen. When you live for the interests of God and others, you automatically participate in the body of Christ, tithe, encourage, and strengthen. Your friends, family, and larger community are blessed because you are around. You become a blessing, a giver, a pillar.

John said very much the same thing in one of his letters. He wrote:

> This is love for God: to obey his commands. And
> his commands are not burdensome, for everyone
> born of God overcomes the world. This is the
> victory that has overcome the world, even our
> faith.
>
> —1 John 5:3–4

To love God is to obey. Note how *un*pessimistic John's tone is here—he's not worried about whether or not obedience to God's commands is possible. He clearly thinks obedience *is* possible, and that is the key to total victory.

The primary idea is repeated in 2 Corinthians 7:1, where Paul writes:

> Since we have these promises, dear friends, let us
> purify ourselves from everything that contami-
> nates body and spirit, perfecting holiness out of
> reverence for God.

Can he possibly mean this? Is this practical? I think so.

Here is how to do it. Think about the things that pollute your body or your spirit, and get rid of them today. Some of you might need to get rid of some things hiding in your home, office, or vehicle. Others of you might need to sever some unholy relationships. Others of you need to clean out your computer and forget some of the Web sites you have been visiting. Others of you need to get into a small group at a good church and develop healthy Christian relationships. Others of you need to stop being crass and rude. Others of you need to reconnect with your wife and kids.

Take an inventory. Do it. Shape up.

Maybe you say you cannot do those things. Maybe you think obedience is out of reach for you. Why? Are you a cow, a pig, or a mosquito? Can't you control yourself at all? Do you live by instincts, or do you have the ability to make decisions? Are you a human being?

If you are human, you can decide. The capacity to change your behavior is within you if you are filled with the Holy Spirit. You have choices to make. You can purify yourself from everything that contaminates your body and spirit, and you can start right now. Do it. Put this book down and do it. And when you do, the natural result will be a refining of God's holiness in your life.

No Obligation to Sin, Whether Young or Old

Some young Christians delay real refinement because they think they have time to get their lives straight. But when Paul wrote to young Timothy, he said:

> The goal of this command is love, which comes
> from a pure heart and a good conscience and a
> sincere faith.
>   —1 Timothy 1:5

Here was an aging man of God exhorting a young man to incredibly high (but very obtainable) ideals: to live a life of love and have:

- A pure heart

- A good conscience

- A sincere faith

If it is possible for Timothy, it is possible for you.

Bottom line: you cannot believe the Bible and say that you have an obligation to sin. In his letter to the church in Rome, Paul says:

> We died to sin; how can we live in it any longer?...
> You have been set free from sin and have become slaves to righteousness. I put this in human terms because you are weak in your natural selves. Just as you used to offer the parts of your body in slavery to impurity and to ever-increasing wickedness, so now offer them in slavery to righteousness leading to holiness.
> —Romans 6:2, 18–19

No questions there—righteousness is our master. We cannot live in sin any longer.

> Therefore, brothers, we have an obligation—but it is not to the sinful nature, to live according to it.
> —Romans 8:12

Clear enough, yes? It would take a worldly Bible scholar to construct the rationale that says we are bound to sin.

Now, don't get me wrong. I do think we will commit individual acts of sin as long as we are in our bodies on the earth. But I know that in the holy place, the percentages are different. Before we come to the altar and the basin, our lives are controlled by sin. Then, as we live in the outer court and are forgiven and baptized, we begin to grow in the power of God. We can struggle and be compelled to sin, but as we approach the holy place, the power of righteousness overwhelms the power of sin, and we find ourselves living in righteousness with sin only entering our lives from time to time. The percentages change.

Walking in obedience lets us into the holy place.

Oh, Really?!

Outer court Christians often think inner court Christians have never been abused, misused, betrayed, hurt, or disappointed because they appear to be so innocent. *They are* childlike, but, in fact, inner court Christians have just discovered a secret that heals, restores, and creates a depth of spirituality that expresses itself in childlike faith.

Entire ministries have been built on the struggles of the outer court, which is fine as long as they don't leave people there. Going into the holy place is a great reward.

Let's obey and go in...to the holy place.

CHAPTER EIGHT

Good Food and Light: How God Satisfies and Directs Us

If you have been a Christian very long, you have seen spiritually hungry people. You see them at church or Bible study, and you wonder if anything will ever satisfy them. They are always excited about some new teacher or teaching, some new revelation or encounter, some new movement of God that is *finally it.* But none of it ever lasts. They have moments of excitement followed by periods of wandering. They are never really full, never really stable. They are always chasing peace and fulfillment.

Such Christians are not weak people. They aren't hopeless. They are just hungry. They need the bread of the presence to sustain them.

We have visited the altar and the basin. We have identified with Christ and have begun to manifest obedience to God. Now, we enter the holy place. To our right, we see a gold-covered table with the bread of the presence on it. To our left, we see the golden lamp stand. Directly in front of us is the altar of incense. All three elements hold key lessons for us as we continue to pursue the good life. We will discuss the altar of incense in a later chapter, but for now, I want us to focus on the bread of the presence and the golden lamp stand.

Why Jesus Chose Bread

The bread of the presence, shown on the facing page, represents the enduring, sustaining presence of God. I believe the bread of the presence may have been what Jesus was thinking of when He ate a meal with His disciples on the night He was arrested. That evening He instituted what we call "the Lord's Supper." He took bread, gave thanks to God for it, broke it, and passed it to His disciples, saying, "Take and eat; this is My body." (See Matthew 26.)

Of course, this symbol of bread was familiar to Jesus' fellow Jews. They knew about the manna God provided for the Israelites in the desert (more on this below). They also knew that in the holy place there was a golden table holding the bread of the presence. On the night of the Last Supper, Jesus might have been referencing that bread—saying that He is the bread of the presence and that we can consume the presence of God.

Jesus referred to Himself as sustaining bread again and again. John 6 recounts the story of Jesus miraculously feeding five thousand people with two pieces of fish and five loaves of bread. With miraculous bread on everyone's mind, Jesus took the opportunity to teach His disciples about the true bread of life.

> "For the bread of God is he who comes down from heaven and gives life to the world." ...Then Jesus declared, "I am the bread of life. He who comes to me will never go hungry, and he who believes in me will never be thirsty."
> —John 6:33, 35

The Table of the Bread of the Presence / The Sustaining,
Enduring Presence of God

He continued by making explicit reference to a bread story they
all knew very well:

> Your forefathers ate the manna in the desert, yet
> they died. But here is the bread that comes down
> from heaven, which a man may eat and not die. I
> am the living bread that came down from heaven.
> If anyone eats of this bread, he will live forever.
> This bread is my flesh, which I will give for the
> life of the world.
>
> —John 6:49–51

Manna was a special food miraculously sent from God to feed
the Israelites after the exodus from Egypt. It was a white substance that resembled frost, took the form of thin flakes, and
tasted like honey. The Bible says:

> When the dew was gone, thin flakes like frost on
> the ground appeared on the desert floor....The
> people of Israel called the bread manna. It was

white like coriander seed and tasted like wafers
made with honey.   —Exodus 16:14, 31

The story of God's provision of manna is something the Jews
celebrated continually. Here, Jesus was extending their understanding of what the manna
meant. He was helping
them see that it was a pre-
view of our dependence on
the sustaining life of Christ.
In Exodus, the children
of Israel relied on God's
provision every single day;
they would have starved to
death in the desert with-
out it. Likewise, believers
in Christ cannot live without consuming Him—taking Him in
and being filled with His presence.

> *God makes His sustaining
> presence available to us, but
> we have to respond obediently
> and responsibly.*

Consume God and Be Filled

The Israelites had to gather their manna six mornings a week
whether they felt like it or not. Likewise, we cannot come to
God only when we want to, or when we are in trouble or pain.
God's provision is about steady, consistent dependence. God is
our food. He sustains us. He is our sustenance.

God provided the manna and made it available to everyone,
but they had to go get it. They had to stoop down and gather it.
Today, God makes His sustaining presence available to us, but we
have to respond obediently and responsibly. We cannot take in the
presence of God by lying in bed all day. We cannot be sustained
by His food if we do not look for it, gather it, and take it in. We
have to choose to rely on Him.

When we pray and worship the Lord in the mornings, we consume Him. When we live well throughout the day, we demonstrate His sustaining life within. When we ingest His nature, His thoughts, His will, His power, His life, and His abilities, we are less likely to deal with guilt and frustration because we have Him on the inside.

We cannot just believe that Jesus satisfies; we actually have to *eat* and be full. We cannot just think about the realities of Scripture; we have to choose to live those realities. We are the living proof of what we believe. We demonstrate it. We cannot just doze in religious reflection; we have to energize ourselves in Him.

Good (and Obedient) Eating Habits

The manna God provided for Israel could be gathered six mornings a week, but not on the seventh. On the sixth day, everyone was to gather twice as much as usual so that they would be prepared for the day of rest when no manna would be provided. Once again, this is a reminder for us of the importance of manifested obedience.

Obedience is not hard, but it does require listening and believing the facts. Every day of the week but Friday, if the people gathered too much, the manna would rot. They could not hoard but could only take as much as they needed on those days. On the other hand, if they neglected to gather as much as they had been told to gather on Friday, they would be hungry on Saturday.

We cannot operate today on the life that we enjoyed yesterday. Every day is new and requires new strength. But there are special times when we are to take a double portion of Christ and enjoy Him during a Sabbath—trusting in Him to sustain us. In obedience, God's life in us does not get old. It does not rot; it does not stink or decay.

These old stories and examples—the bread in the inner taber-nacle, manna in the desert—were very familiar to Jesus' disciples and followers. As He spoke about Himself as the bread of life, the images from these old stories ran through their heads and took on new meanings. Jesus wanted them to know that if they ate of Him, they would never be hungry again.

Plain White Bread

Bread can be a delicacy—stuffed with rosemary and olives, sprin-kled with sea salt, dipped in balsamic vinegar and olive oil—but it is often a regular, casual food.

Certainly for the Hebrew people in the desert, bread was some-thing ordinary, not exceptional. It was not an expensive, rare treat. It was an everyday, basic food.

The presence of God is a precious, holy, sometimes frightening thing. But the bread of the presence suggests another side of the presence of God, which is the abiding Spirit that is with us day in and day out, whether we are attending a worship service or going to the bank.

When I think of eating bread, I calm down. I slow down. I trust. I know I can depend upon His nature and character to see me through. The idea of consuming the bread of the pres-ence takes pressure off of me and causes me to rest, knowing that a steady, consistent life in Christ is what He has provided for me. Bread is nutritious but not fancy. It is common, steady, trustworthy.

Because of the bread of life, I can go to Christian conferences and enjoy them, but I do not feel the need to go to them in order to straighten my life out every six months. Because of the bread, I am OK with serving in a humble role in my local church and my family without the pressure to prove something. Because of the bread of life, I am not under pressure to have a powerful encounter every time I read my Bible or pray. I trust God. I do not need to have an inspired word to get me through every day. With the bread in my life, I am consistent and trustworthy. I am a steady pillar. I am predictable. With the bread of the presence inside me, I am safe, sated, satisfied.

One Loaf, One Body

When Paul commented on the Lord's Supper, he said:

> And is not the bread that we break a participation in the body of Christ? Because there is one loaf, we, who are many, are one body, for we all partake of the one loaf.
> —1 Corinthians 10:16–17

Here Paul is highlighting several big ideas:

Bread provides nutrition for every part of our bodies, and bread takes time to ingest.

We don't eat bread one moment and experience hunger soon after; instead, it is a sustaining nutrient. So is Christ. When we are in the holy place eating the bread of the presence, we are consuming Christ in a stable, steady, long-lasting way that will impact every portion of our lives. His personality, nature, name, power, and authority are being inculcated into every cell in our bodies. His presence comes into us in a special, abiding way, and, as a result, the promises of God come alive in us naturally.

When we participate in the body of Christ, we can receive healing.

The Bible teaches this in both the Old Testament and the New. In Isaiah 53:5, the Bible says:

> But he was pierced for our transgressions, he was crushed for our iniquities; the punishment

that brought us peace was upon him, and by his wounds we are healed.

In 1 Peter 2:24, Peter repeats this idea, saying:

He himself bore our sins in his body on the tree, so that we might die to sins and live for righteousness; by his wounds you have been healed.

There is one body, even though there are many members.

Here Paul is emphasizing that we are assimilated into a body where each one of us is just a member. In Romans 12:4–5, Paul writes:

Just as each of us has one body with many members, and these members do not all have the same function, so in Christ we who are many form one body, and each member belongs to all the others.

As I have said, in order for us to fulfill our micronarrative, we have to acknowledge and participate within the metanarrative. We might be a heart, a tongue, a nose, or a brain, but however special our role, our purpose is to serve the whole.

There is one Christ, from whom we must all eat.

Jesus is the full revelation of God, which is why it is crucial for us to not slip into just talking about "God" as a generic concept. Jesus Himself—the very person who lived as a human in the Middle East some two thousand years ago—is whom we must consume. Jesus is God; He is our focus, and His is the life we must ingest.

Eating the bread of life, the bread of the presence in the holy place, brings stability and integrity because it is singular; it is one loaf. In eating it we are part of a body that is single, one, unified. No longer are we unstable, seeking, dissatisfied, always looking for a better Bible teacher or someone with a greater anointing.

We are not nervous or restless anymore. We are full, and we enjoy rest in His presence. This bread, Jesus Himself, is our sustenance for life.

Leave the Light On

Now, the lamp stand.

Inside the holy place, the lamp stand to our left is a big one. Refer to the illustration below for a detailed view. It is made of

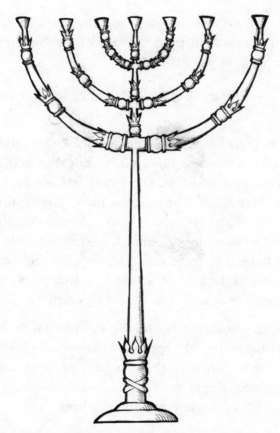

The Lampstand / Bright Actions and Walking in the Light

pure gold—seventy-five pounds' worth. It features depictions of flower cups, buds, and blossoms. Six branches extend from the sides of the lamp stand, three on each side with the seventh in the middle. The lamp stand is a work of art. It is costly. The seven candlesticks are a perfect number, and their flames burn simultaneously, demonstrating the perfect fire of God working in the life of the worshiper.

I believe that Jesus was thinking of the lamp stand when He said, "I am the light of the world" (John 8:12).

Matthew quotes the prophet Isaiah when referencing Jesus as the light of the world:

> The people living in darkness have seen a great light; on those living in the land of the shadow of death a light has dawned.　　—Matthew 4:16

In John 1:4–9, the Bible again describes Jesus as our light. It says:

> In him was life, and that life was the light of men. The light shines in the darkness, but the darkness has not understood it. There came a man who was sent from God; his name was John [the Baptist]. He came as a witness to testify concerning that light, so that through him all men might believe. He himself was not the light; he came only as a witness to the light. The true light that gives light to every man was coming into the world.

Just as Jesus was present with us at the altar in His sacrifice, at the basin by promising His Spirit and the water of life, and at the table by being the bread of the presence, so He is also the light of the lamp stand. Really, the tabernacle is all about Jesus and the various ways He enters into and fills our lives.

Bright Actions

If you read the opening chapters of Genesis, you will see that Adam and Eve had to choose between the tree of the knowledge of good and evil and the tree of life. I think this is the struggle that continues today. We have to decide if our spirituality is going to be based on knowledge about what is good and what is evil, or if it is going to be rooted in godly innocence. Even though the habit of choosing goodness is, well, good, it is not necessarily godly. Godly goodness comes from the life of God being imparted into us as our old nature dies and Christ's goodness is manifested.

If we do not know any better, we will study and learn about good things to do, try to avoid evil things, and hopefully act in a godly way. That may be a wholesome life, but it lacks power. Our lives are transformed only by partaking of the life of God Himself. Only by relying on Jesus can His light shine through us.

> *We have to decide if our spirituality is going to be based on knowledge about what is good and what is evil, or if it is going to be rooted in godly innocence.*

Jesus said to the Jewish leaders of His day:

> You diligently study the Scriptures because you think that by them you possess eternal life. These are the Scriptures that testify about me, yet you refuse to come to me to have life.
>
> —John 5:39–40

Notice this! The author of Scripture Himself is saying that the point of the Scripture is to find Him. If we do, then His light shines in our lives.

Jesus said:

> I am the light of the world. Whoever follows me
> will never walk in darkness, but will have the light
> of life.
>
> —John 8:12

There is no need to lack confidence in who we are or where we are going. Christians are not in the dark, and they never need act as if they are unclear on God's purposes for them in the world. Not only do we *know* the light, but also we *are* the light for our generation.

Matthew 5:14–16 says this in perfect clarity:

> You are the light of the world. A city on a hill
> cannot be hidden. Neither do people light a lamp
> and put it under a bowl. Instead they put it on its
> stand, and it gives light to everyone in the house.
> In the same way, let your light shine before men,
> that they may see your good deeds and praise your
> Father in heaven.

Jesus has given you life in order to show you off. This world is dark, and He wants to put you in positions to shine brightly. So when we are in holy place living, doors will supernaturally open. God will see that His wisdom and knowledge are alive and operational in you, and your light can shine brighter than you ever imagined. God will produce good works in you that will draw people to Him.

So, how do we let light shine? We act like Christians. We act differently from other people because we have been through something incredible—we have received the good life of God.

Darkness Is Not Light

Christians are faced with a tricky challenge—how do we reach into the darkness and still remain in the light? And if we are spending all of our time thinking about the darkness, is it even possible to stay lit? I have seen it time and time again—Christians trying desperately to be cool and falling into the darkness under the guise of reaching others. When we appease darkness, we are no longer light.

> This is the verdict: Light has come into the world, but men loved darkness instead of light because their deeds were evil. Everyone who does evil hates the light, and will not come into the light for fear that his deeds will be exposed. But whoever lives by the truth comes into the light, so that it may be seen plainly that what he has done has been done through God.
>
> —John 3:19–21

We are not light because we are nice, smiley people. We are light because God's life has transformed us.

In Galatians 5:22–23, the apostle Paul explains what our life looks like when we are dominated by the Holy Spirit. He lists the characteristics of people who have consumed God and walked into this light. I have listed them here for you with comment, hoping to explain in practical terms how our lives become light.

- *Love: Living for the good of another.* While the rest of the world is living for itself, we shock the world by taking care of, defending, and protecting others. When we are focused on others, we are demonstrating love.

- *Joy: Knowing your purpose.* As we grow in God's plan for our lives, we begin to flow in God's purpose. There's nothing more joy-producing than that. The definition of satisfaction is fulfilling the purpose for which you were created.

- *Peace: Trusting in His character.* I have said it before and I will say it throughout my life: being a Christian is easy. It is letting go of the resistance and relaxing to believe in God. I know God is good, loving, merciful, gracious, compassionate, patient, true, faithful, and just. Because of this, I can lean back into His arms and rest in who He is. Knowing God is a huge sigh of relief.

- *Patience: Believing time is your friend.* I believe that I should only be in a hurry about one thing: winning the lost. Other than that, I need to work hard six days a week and rest on the seventh. Within this context, I can be patient, because what I am doing is just a part of God's metanarrative.

- *Kindness: Caring for the feelings of others.* There is no reason to be rude to people or to treat them as if they are the product of natural selection. They are not. They are human beings made in the image and likeness of God. Whether they have discovered God's plan for their lives or not, they deserve dignity and our respect.

- *Goodness: Being trustworthy.* Goodness means my character is not determined by my circumstances or the actions of others. I am who I am, and I am determined to treat others well. People can trust me to behave in a godly, consistent manner no matter what. That's goodness.

- *Faithfulness: Living our core.* Faithfulness is steadiness, consistency, and dependable loyalty.

When our core has been transformed and we have settled our convictions, all we have to do is be faithful to that core.

- *Gentleness: Responding to human frailty with grace.* Gentleness is patience in action; it responds with a soft voice or a soft presence. Gentleness provides understanding and comfort.

- *Self-control: Staying steady.* Every single day, I am the same person. Sure, there are various sides of my personality, but I do not wrestle with who I should be. I know what I should do and what I shouldn't do. I keep my feet on the ground, flee temptation when it comes, and resist the devil. With God's help, I can withstand temptation and control my actions. I am a Christian, and I live like a Christian.

As we actively exhibit these godly characteristics, we are light. Every one of these demonstrations of God's grace in our lives dispels the darkness. We have been transformed. With the bread of the presence sustaining us and the lamp stand lighting us at all times, we are people of God doing the work of God. It's a great life.

CHAPTER NINE

The Good Confidence: Why We Can Trust God's Love

I hope you are not tired of me saying this, because here it comes again: Christian living is easy.

Now, understand, I've been through years of struggle against my own sinfulness. But I have persevered in my determination to ask forgiveness, grow in God's Word, memorize the Scriptures, have honest connectivity with my wife and friends, and pray and fast. I tithe and try to grow in love and godly living. I have no doubt that God has forgiven me, protected me, shielded me, covered for me, drawn me, and had compassion toward me in every way.

I have had to face temptation and trials along the way, but I have seen God prevail.

We will have complications, hang-ups, and even some failures, but God will win, and He wants you to win, too.

That's why it is easy to be a Christian. God pulls you along. God gives you strength. The Bible says that Jesus intercedes on your behalf, which means He is cheering you on and providing help in every moment.

If these things are true, and they are, then who wouldn't agree that being a Christian can be easy? We have everything working in our favor.

Manifesting obedience demonstrates that the blood and water have, in fact, transformed you. In the holy place, you have become steady, stable, and consistent because of the impact of the bread, His body, in every area of your life. As a result, perfect light and life are working in and through you, the lamp stand.

> *Confidence does not mean arrogance, self-righteousness, or ignorance of the seriousness of sinfulness....It is confidence in God, not in ourselves.*

Now, step forward into the middle of the holy place. In front of you is the altar of incense, which we will look at in the next chapter. Behind you to your right is the bread, and to your left is the lamp stand. Now, you can experience total security, confidence, trust, intimacy, oneness, and safety in Him. In this place, you are in His perfect sanctuary from the negative effects of sin and the world. You are arriving.

Confident, Secure, and at Rest

One of my favorite Christian paradoxes is that we should be simultaneously humble and confident before God. Humility doesn't exactly come easy, but you can intellectually ascertain that it is appropriate to be humble before the God of the universe. But here's the paradox: God's love and mercy are so extravagant, they are so all-encompassing, that we can be confident as we approach Him, too.

The writer of Hebrews says:

Nothing in all creation is hidden from God's sight. Everything is uncovered and laid bare before the eyes of him to whom we must give account. Therefore, since we have a great high priest who has gone through the heavens, Jesus the Son of God, let us hold firmly to the faith we profess. For we do not have a high priest who is unable to sympathize with our weaknesses, but we have one who has been tempted in every way, just as we are—yet was without sin. Let us then approach the throne of grace with confidence, so that we may receive mercy and find grace to help us in our time of need.

—Hebrews 4:13–16

Christian teachers have quoted this remarkable passage for centuries, and with good reason. It tells us that God sees everything—He knows every thought, every action at every moment of our days—but nonetheless, we can approach Him with confidence. We can *know* He will give us grace. That's how much He loves us.

Confidence does not mean arrogance, self-righteousness, or ignorance of the seriousness of sinfulness. It means that when we approach the throne of grace, we can have assurance that Christ's blood and Spirit are in us and have done their work. It is confidence in God, not in ourselves.

His intent was that now, through the church, the manifold wisdom of God should be made known to the rulers and authorities in the heavenly realms, according to his eternal purpose which he accomplished in Christ Jesus our Lord. In him and through faith in him we may approach God with freedom and confidence.

—Ephesians 3:10–12

> Therefore, brothers, since we have confidence to
> enter the Most Holy Place by the blood of Jesus,
> by a new and living way opened for us through
> the curtain, that is, his body, and since we have
> a great priest over the house of God, let us draw
> near to God with a sincere heart in full assurance
> of faith, having our hearts sprinkled to cleanse us
> from a guilty conscience and having our bodies
> washed with pure water.   —Hebrews 10:19–22

Reading over these verses, it is not hard to see why this is a tough sell, and why some people remain in the outer court most of their lives. The fact that we can have this much confidence before God is nothing short of a miracle. But it is a miracle that God has provided and one that we absolutely must accept. The apostle John says:

> In this way, love is made complete among us so
> that we will have confidence on the day of judg-
> ment, because in this world we are like him.
>   —1 John 4:17

Think of that! He is saying that we don't have to fear eternal judgment. Sounds like assurance of holy place living to me. Later, he writes:

> This is the confidence we have in approaching
> God: that if we ask anything according to his will,
> he hears us. And if we know that he hears us—
> whatever we ask—we know that we have what we
> asked of him.   —1 John 5:14–15

Could it be more clear? We should humble ourselves before God, but we can do it confidently. That's a paradox, but it is one that we should embrace. When we do, it leads us straight into the good life.

Six Pictures of Security

One way to gain confidence in God is to meditate on and really grasp the total reality of who you are in Him. Earlier, I listed various attributes of our identity in Christ from Neil Anderson and gave you several scriptures to this end. Now, let's look at six pictures the Bible offers to showcase our security in God.

1. We are God's fellow workers.

First Corinthians 3:9 says:

> For we are God's fellow workers; you are God's field, God's building.

Paul is saying that we work along with God in this world. We have the responsibility to cultivate people just as a farmer cultivates a field in order to make it productive, which means we must understand the way seasons work in people's lives. We also have a responsibility to build people into God's plan just as a builder would put various pieces into place in order to construct a functional building. Both the farmer and the builder are professionals in what they do. They are skillful and, because of their work, food and shelter are provided. Likewise, we feed and protect people when we see ourselves as God's fellow workers.

2. We are sheep.

Hebrews 13:20–21 says:

> May the God of peace, who through the blood of the eternal covenant brought back from the dead our Lord Jesus, that great Shepherd of the sheep, equip you with everything good for doing his will.

Jesus our Shepherd equips us with everything we need in order to accomplish His will. Shepherds are gentle, compassionate, and protective of their sheep, and so is God toward us.

3. We are members of a body.

First Corinthians 12:12 says:

> The body is a unit, though it is made up of many
> parts; and though all its parts are many, they form
> one body. So it is with Christ.

The Bible illustrates that we are each one part of a whole. Each member of the body receives its significance by virtue of the overall purpose of the body. As a body member, we cannot be disconnected (unless we intentionally disconnect ourselves). Even if we are temporarily weak or frail, we can recover and still be a strong member.

4. We are Christ's bride.

We are His desired companion, His lover, His co-worker, His intimate partner. We are the one He wants to live with, work with, rest with, process with, and grow with through the years. He wants to provide for us, protect us, work in cooperation with us, and lead us. Revelation 19:7 says:

> Let us rejoice and be glad and give him glory! For
> the wedding of the Lamb has come, and his bride
> has made herself ready.

We have made ourselves ready for Christ through accepting what He has done for us and living in obedience. Every wife loves resting in the security of her husband's love, just as we can find rest in the security of Jesus' love. We don't need to strive for it. It's there.

5. We are God's children.

We have been adopted by a loving heavenly father. First John 3:1 says:

> How great is the love the Father has lavished on
> us, that we should be called children of God! And

that is what we are! The reason the world does not
know us is that it did not know him.

I love giving my kids things, just as God does. I also love training and disciplining my children so they can be responsible adults,
just as God does. Even though there are days when I am dis-
pleased with my children, they are mine, always will be mine, and
can never be anything but my children. That is the way God feels
about us. We are in His family, and He is pleased with that.

6. We are God's dwelling.

In the Old Testament, God resided in the holy of holies. Now His
Spirit lives in us individually and corporately as we are connected
together as His body. Ephesians 2:21–22 says:

> In him the whole building is joined together and
> rises to become a holy temple in the Lord. And in
> him you too are being built together to become a
> dwelling in which God lives by his Spirit.

We are each a piece of the overall structure. A beam, a pipe, or
a foundation stone isn't nervous about its role. Once placed, it
just does it. God is placing you in your role right now, and as you
are placed, you may rest in Him.

All these images should give us assurance, freedom, and confidence. Grasping these pictures should help us read the scriptures
about God's chosen people and know, without hesitation, that
they are talking about us.

Who You Are in the Holy Place

In this next section, I will reference several verses that describe
who you are in the holy place. I won't comment too heavily
because I want you to meditate on these verses. The ideas speak
for themselves, so it is up to you to let them sink into you.

Let's begin by looking at two verses that are clearly about you. Both are from Paul's letter to the Ephesians.

In Ephesians chapter 1, Paul writes about the church. He says:

> For he chose us in him before the creation of the world to be holy and blameless in his sight. In love he predestined us to be adopted as his sons through Jesus Christ, in accordance with his pleasure and will—to the praise of his glorious grace, which he has freely given us in the One he loves.
> —Ephesians 1:4–6

A few sentences later, Paul continues:

> In him we were also chosen, having been predestined according to the plan of him who works out everything in conformity with the purpose of his will, in order that we, who were the first to hope in Christ, might be for the praise of his glory.
> —Ephesians 1:11–12

Remember, these verses are in reference to you. If you are not familiar with the major terms here, I suggest you purchase a good study Bible and read the footnotes on these verses. They will encourage you and give you the freedom, confidence, and security necessary to approach the altar of incense with a clean conscience and a pure heart.

Jesus Himself entered the holy place on our behalf, and He's calling you to join Him. In Hebrews 6:17–20, the Bible says:

> Because God wanted to make the unchanging nature of his purpose very clear to the heirs of what was promised, he confirmed it with an oath. God did this so that, by two unchangeable things in which it is impossible for God to lie, we who have fled to take hold of the hope offered to us

may be greatly encouraged. We have this hope as
an anchor for the soul, firm and secure. It enters
the inner sanctuary behind the curtain, where
Jesus, who went before us, has entered on our
behalf.

You are the "heir of what was promised." You are running to
take hold of the hope that has been offered. We have a hope that
is not flimsy, but rather an anchor for our souls. It is firm and
secure. Jesus wants us in the holy place with Him. It is your name
He's calling. He wants you.

Accepting your place in God involves a kind of growth process.
Paul highlights this in Romans, where he writes:

> And we know that in all things God works for the
> good of those who love him, who have been called
> according to his purpose. For those God foreknew
> he also predestined to be conformed to the like-
> ness of his Son, that he might be the firstborn
> among many brothers. And those he predestined,
> he also called; those he called, he also justified;
> those he justified, he also glorified.
>   —Romans 8:28–30

The main idea here is that your place in God is sure. Paul loved
this assurance so much that in his next sentence, he exclaimed:

> What, then, shall we say in response to this? If
> God is for us, who can be against us?
>   —Romans 8:31

The promise is only for those who love Him and have been
called according to His purpose. That's you. That process has
happened to you. And since it is you, God will work everything
in your life for your good.

Your life is no longer random. God sees every situation, and He
will give you wisdom. You can be confident. Don't be passive—

be actively involved in His plan for your life, and you will see His plan unfold.

Jesus said:

> Come to me, all you who are weary and burdened, and I will give you rest. Take my yoke upon you and learn from me, for I am gentle and humble in heart, and you will find rest for your souls. For my yoke is easy and my burden is light.
> —Matthew 11:28–30

Easy and light. See—the "Christianity is easy" idea didn't start with me! Most Christians (again, my guess would be about 94 percent) have not experienced this stage of Christian living. They have not enjoyed rest or security. Why? Either because they are staying in the outer court or because they have decided to go home.

If you are in the outer court (or have left the journey of faith completely), turn toward the holy place by manifesting the obedience God has seeded inside your heart. Become stable and consistent with the bread of the presence. Let the light of life begin to shine through you. Then, as you walk toward the altar of incense, let the freedom, confidence, and assurance of your calling develop in you. Study the scriptures I have mentioned here. Rest.

Most Christians have not enjoyed rest or security. Why? Either because they are staying in the outer court or because they have decided to go home.

Relax. Gain assurance. Then worship and pray like never before.

We are safe in him. Jesus said, "And this is the will of him who sent me, that I shall lose none of all that he has given me, but raise them up at the last day" (John 6:39).

Jesus also said:

> My sheep listen to my voice; I know them, and
> they follow me. I give them eternal life, and they
> shall never perish; no one can snatch them out of
> my hand. My Father, who has given them to me,
> is greater than all; no one can snatch them out of
> my Father's hand.
>
> —John 10:27–29

Read those verses again and again. They are promises for you!
Want more evidence of security and freedom? How about
Romans 8:38–39, where Paul writes:

> For I am convinced that neither death nor life,
> neither angels nor demons, neither the present
> nor the future, nor any powers, neither height nor
> depth, nor anything else in all creation, will be
> able to separate us from the love of God that is in
> Christ Jesus our Lord.

In the holy place, when adversity comes our way, we draw closer to Christ. In the outer court, many who have adversity actually draw away from Christ in confusion, doubt, and foolishness. Not so in the holy place. In the holy place, we trust Him, we know Him, and we rest in the fact that He has chosen us and will faithfully complete the work He has begun in us.

Now, in confidence, let's go to the altar of incense.

CHAPTER TEN

The Good Listener: How God Hears Us

A quick recap:

We have been to the outer court with the bronze altar for forgiveness of sins and the bronze basin for water and Spirit baptism. Both reminded us of Christ's identification with our humanity.

In the holy place, we identified with Christ and died to ourselves. Obedience became the norm. We visited the table holding the bread of the presence. We partook of that bread and were sustained by the life of Jesus. We became stable, predictable, and deeply satisfied in Him. Then we visited the lamp stand, where Jesus, the light of the world, became light in us so we could be His light for our generation.

Then, with the assurance that can only come from total dependence upon Christ's work on the cross, we rested in confidence. Rest, for the first time in our walk with God, became our dominant characteristic.

Now we begin to find out what the tabernacle is really for: the glory of God.

In rest, confidence, security, and absolute assurance, we step forward to the altar of incense. Here we speak to God in thanksgiving and prayer, and He listens and responds to our prayers. Even our thoughts instantly become answered prayers. Here, the promises are fulfilled. At the altar of incense, communication with God is instantaneous and answers are instant. Communication is perfect.

The Burning Incense of Prayer

The close-up illustration of the golden altar of incense in the tabernacle, shown below, reveals that it burned with beautiful fragrances that symbolized the continual worship and prayers of

The Altar of Incense / Effective Prayer and Worship

God's people. This is but one of many places in the Bible where incense symbolizes prayer. It is a powerful symbol: just as the smoke lifts from the altar and floats toward heaven, so our prayers lift from our lips and float to the ear of God.

The Bible says:

> And when he had taken [the scroll], the four living creatures and the twenty-four elders fell down before the Lamb. Each one had a harp and they were holding golden bowls full of incense, which are the prayers of the saints.
> —Revelation 5:8

Later, the apostle John uses this image once again:

> Another angel, who had a golden censer [or bowl], came and stood at the altar. He was given much incense to offer, with the prayers of all the saints, on the golden altar before the throne. The smoke of the incense, together with the prayers of the saints, went up before God from the angel's hand.
> —Revelation 8:3–4

I love this image of God accumulating prayers in a bowl in heaven. To extrapolate, I believe that when great numbers of people pray, and when people persevere in prayer, there comes a time when the bowls fill and the answers flow out to the earth. More and more prayer equals more and more fragrant incense wafting toward the heavens. That is why I have spent my life encouraging people to pray as much as possible.

Prayer impacts everything. Yes, *everything*. Prayer is *not* just the verbal attempt of sinful people trying to get their sins forgiven. It is a significant interaction between God and His people that shifts the course of human events. As we seek God's will and pray in the holy place, we play a role in God's ministry to the people of the earth.

Does God Always Respond?

Holy place worship and prayer are consumed with God and His purposes on the earth. It is serious business. Still, holy place prayers can be easy, conversational prayers. God wants to listen, and He does not make it hard on us. A humble but confident exchange can take place at the altar of incense.

People raise their eyebrows when we talk about God not responding to prayer. The wisdom of the day, in both religious and secular circles, is that God responds well to people as long as they are "sincere." But sincerity is only one ingredient. God has established a clear protocol for human beings to approach and pray before Him. Anyone is welcome to approach, but they must meet God's criteria.

Prayer is not just the verbal attempt of sinful people trying to get their sins forgiven. It is a significant interaction between God and His people that shifts the course of human events.

Worship and prayer at the altar of incense are totally different from outer court prayer. They are committed to the glory of God, and they come from hearts dedicated to holiness. In Psalm 66:17–20, the psalmist writes:

> I cried out to him with my mouth; his praise was on my tongue. If I had cherished sin in my heart, the Lord would not have listened; but God has surely listened and heard my voice in prayer. Praise be to God, who has not rejected my prayer or withheld his love from me!

This psalm suggests some uncomfortable possibilities: that God can choose not to listen to us, and that He can reject our prayers and withhold His love. Holiness matters to Him, which is why active, manifested obedience is so crucial for holy place living.

Isaiah also cautions us about the risk of mute prayers:

> Stop bringing meaningless offerings! Your incense is detestable to me. New Moons, Sabbaths and convocations—I cannot bear your evil assemblies. Your New Moon festivals and your appointed feasts my soul hates. They have become a burden to me; I am weary of bearing them. When you spread out your hands in prayer, I will hide my eyes from you; even if you offer many prayers, I will not listen. Your hands are full of blood; wash and make yourselves clean. Take your evil deeds out of my sight! Stop doing wrong, learn to do right! Seek justice, encourage the oppressed. Defend the cause of the fatherless, plead the case of the widow.
>
> —Isaiah 1:13–17

The point? Outer court living does not mix with holy place worship and prayer. Wrestling with temptation, constant need for repentance from willful sin, quenching the flow of God's Spirit—this is not stuff that necessarily causes God to reject us eternally, but it is stuff that makes our prayers ineffective.

I do not mean this teaching to be especially hard, nor do I mean it to be spooky. It is just a real warning from the Scriptures. God wants us to pray, and He wants us to pray specifically and actively about urgent matters facing our generation. But He wants us to pray from a position of reverence and holiness—which is to say, at the altar of incense in the holy place.

Promises Fulfilled

It is at the altar of incense where God's promises to us are answered. This is the place where scriptures are fulfilled in our lives, promises and assurances given by the Holy Spirit are realized, and oneness with the Father is as close as is possible on this side of heaven.

At the altar of incense, communication, oneness, and awe wrap in innocence in the presence of God. It's here where the scripture in Mark 11:24 is fulfilled:

> Therefore I tell you, whatever you ask for in prayer, believe that you have received it, and it will be yours.

When at the altar of incense, words must be guarded, thoughts must be focused, and hearts must be consumed in the majesty of His presence. Here, all prayers are answered and the anointing is tender. Here, the voice of God is clear, the power of God is obvious, and the terror and judgment of God are horrifyingly close. Miracles always happen here. Be careful.

At the Altar Every Day

At this point, I am tempted to tell stories about the most dramatic prayer experiences I have had. But I don't think I will do that here. My hesitation is that the stories will tempt you to try to have similar dramatic experiences. Testimony is important, and dramatic encounters are desirable and impacting, but I think it is more important to tell you about the *routine* of holy place prayer. I want to emphasize the daily, regular, and habitual worship and prayer that are characteristic of holy place living.

Altar of incense prayer is not super-spiritual. It *is* deeply spiritual, of course, but it is also regular and habitual.

When I wake up in the morning, the first thing I do is read my Bible. While reading, I make note of the big ideas that stand out to me. After reading a few chapters of the Bible and noting some ideas, I pray for a while.

I pattern my prayer time after what I think Paul was talking about in 1 Corinthians 14:15. There, he writes:

> So what shall I do? I will pray with my spirit, but
> I will also pray with my mind; I will sing with my
> spirit, but I will also sing with my mind.

Although the context here is the role of prophecy and tongues in the public worship service, I think this tells us a lot about the way Paul prayed. Since he is the strongest influence in the formation of the New Testament church after the ascension of the Lord Jesus, I want to model my prayer life after him.

So every day, I do what Paul did. For a little while, I pray with my spirit (more about this below). Then I pray with my mind about varieties of issues. Sometimes I pray through whatever is happening in the news—local, national, and world issues. I pray for my leaders—the president and vice president, my governor and mayor, and so on. I pray for my family, for my friends, for the various ministries at our church, and all the local churches in our area.

Many Christians complicate this kind of prayer. They get caught up with wondering how long they should pray, how many times they should pray for the same thing, whom and what they should pray for on given days of the week. I don't worry about any of that. I just pray for the people, places, and things on my heart.

Another Language of Prayer

Remember, Paul says he prays with his spirit. Even though we can pray in our own language dominated by the Holy Spirit, and that is certainly "praying in the Spirit," I don't think that is what

Paul is talking about here. I think he is talking about praying in a prayer language—a language from God that no human can understand.

When God first formed the church after Jesus ascended into heaven, He gave believers the gift of tongues. When the Holy Spirit first came to believers in Acts 2, they "were filled with the Holy Spirit and began to speak in other tongues as the Spirit enabled them" (v. 4). Outsiders from other nations said they heard them "declaring the wonders of God in [their] own tongues" (v. 11). At this point, God miraculously enabled the disciples to speak in foreign languages they had not learned. That is one form of speaking in tongues.

Another form is mentioned by Paul in 1 Corinthians. There, Paul is contrasting prophecy (saying what God says) with tongues (the Holy Spirit praying and worshiping through a believer). He writes:

> For anyone who speaks in a tongues does not speak to men but to God. Indeed, no one understands him; he utters mysteries with his spirit.
> —1 Corinthians 14:2

When Paul writes that no one understands him, he means that he is speaking out mysteries with his spirit. I think that is also why Paul writes to the Romans:

> In the same way, the Spirit helps us in our weakness. We do not know what we ought to pray for, but the Spirit himself intercedes for us with groans that words cannot express. And he who searches our hearts knows the mind of the Spirit, because the Spirit intercedes for the saints in accordance with God's will.
> —Romans 8:26–27

So the Holy Spirit is able to pray God's perfect will through us. How does the Spirit pray through the believer? Either by dominating our prayers in our native language or by having us pray in tongues.

I received my prayer language years ago, so when I pray alone in the mornings, I pray in the Spirit (tongues) and in the understanding (English). When I do this, my spirit is strengthened and empowered.

> He who speaks in a tongue edifies himself...
> —1 Corinthians 14:4

Next, I soak in the Word and pray about the big ideas from the Bible that I noted earlier. As I pray, I also worship and sing. It is perfectly natural for us to sing in English and sing in the Spirit, just as it was for the apostle Paul.

I know some people teach that this kind of thing doesn't happen anymore. Wrong. There is nothing in either the Bible or in church history that would indicate that the gifts of the Spirit are no longer operational or that they operate differently today than they did in the early church. It takes a religious scholar to explain why the gifts don't operate today, just as it took a religious scholar in Jesus' day to explain why Jesus wasn't the Messiah.

Don't rely on the machinations of scholars who are not comfortable with spiritual experiences. Believe your Bible! Read it yourself. And enjoy praying and singing in the Spirit.

Flowing in the Spirit

No doubt about it, prayer and worship in the Spirit happen in the outer court at the bronze basin when people are baptized in the Holy Spirit. So, what is the difference between doing it there and doing it in the holy place? The difference is what I call "flow." It is a subtlety, a shift in feeling, but it is a crucial difference.

In the outer court, we need to pray in the Spirit because we are desperate for spiritual strength. We pray in the midst of an internal battle, and our spiritual battling rescues us from falling into despair (and yes, of course it is much better for us to fight the battle than to give up).

But at the altar of incense, prayer and worship are a river of life to God that blesses Him and does the work of His kingdom. Here, prayer is His Spirit of intercession and worship working in us and flowing into the heavenly realms. It is an easy flow of life, inspiration, illumination, and power. In the outer court, it is more desperate. In the holy place, it is restful.

While praying in the Spirit and the understanding, sometimes the gift of prophecy will work in me. When this happens, I actually prophesy to myself. I know this seems strange, but I talk to God, and then I am able to say what God is saying back to me. This gives me opportunity to have a conversation with God that is substantive for my natural ears. I speak to God, and I verbalize what God is saying back to me. In this, I am able to carry on a conversation.

> *There is nothing in either the Bible or in church history that would indicate that the gifts of the Spirit are no longer operational or that they operate differently today than they did in the early church.*

This phenomenon requires an understanding of the voice of God and the gift of prophecy. But at the altar of incense, it is natural. I have seen people try this when they are still in the outer court, and it is often polluted. No question, it is good to learn how to operate in the gifts of the Spirit, and it is better to learn the gifts in the privacy of your prayer closet than in public. But know that when you are in the outer court, the chances of your spiritual experience being polluted are much higher than if you are in the holy place at the altar of incense. So obey God, live in the holy place, and practice the gifts of the Spirit.

Not only can you operate in the prophetic while at the altar of incense, but you can also interpret your tongue. Every time I do this, I am informed about what my spirit has been praying. Remember, the Spirit makes intercession for the saints in accordance with God's perfect will. Wouldn't you like to know what the Spirit of God is praying through you?

Paul is clear on this issue. When we pray in tongues, our minds are "unfruitful." In other words, we do not understand what we are saying because tongues is our spiritual language speaking to God. To inform our minds, we need to interpret our prayer in the Spirit—just as, in a church service, a message in tongues would need to be interpreted so everyone could appreciate it. But simply by praying in the Spirit, our spirits are strengthened. We become spiritually stronger when the Holy Spirit prays through us.

I know, some of you are scratching your heads here. Paul explains it all in 1 Corinthians, and churches all over the world practice these concepts. But if these concepts are hurdles you cannot get over, don't let them become stumbling blocks. You can, with your intellect, study the Bible, apply its principles, and live God's plan for your life. Many Christians live a satisfying life this way. If you can do that and continue to really grow in God, do it.

But if you would like more spiritual depth and enlightenment in the Word of God and the power of the Spirit, earnestly desire spiritual gifts. Receive them at the bronze basin in the outer court, and let their power flow at the golden altar of incense in the holy place.

Praying God's Word, Becoming God's Word

As I mentioned earlier, during my time of prayer I pray about "big ideas" that I read in the Bible earlier that morning. I think this too is a powerful experience, and I think it helps me really absorb the principles of God's Word.

> For the word of God is living and active. Sharper than any double-edged sword, it penetrates even to dividing soul and spirit, joints and marrow; it judges the thoughts and attitudes of the heart.
> —Hebrews 4:12

> All Scripture is God-breathed and is useful for teaching, rebuking, correcting and training in righteousness, so that the man of God may be thoroughly equipped for every good work.
> —2 Timothy 3:16–17

Because of these assurances, when I pray, I pray through the big ideas from the Bible, and the Scriptures come alive in me. In some supernatural way, a transition occurs: I move from just believing in the Scriptures to actually becoming them.

Let me give you an example. Let's say I read, "Honor your father and your mother, so that you may live long in the land the LORD your God is giving you" (Exod. 20:12). When I read this, I believe it. I underline it because it is meaningful to me. But just because I believe it and actually value it, that doesn't mean it is *in* me. I believe it and want to obey it, but in my heart, I still might be rebellious or resentful against my parents.

When we read the Bible, we try to submit to God's Word and obey it. We strive to understand it more and more. But when we *pray* His Word, God breathes it into us, and we actually become the principle we are reading about. Then, at our very core, we are not rebellious and resentful. God's Word has transformed our core.

So in prayer, the reality of the Scriptures is written on our hearts. It is not a struggle to obey God's Word; it is a delight, because His Word has transformed us. This process is part of the answer to Jesus' prayer in John 17:17, where He prays, "Sanctify them by the truth; your word is truth."

I do not mean to imply that the Word of God only sanctifies us if we are praying the Word. That's not true. Anytime we spend time in the Word with submitted hearts and minds, the Lord can set us apart for life-giving service. But in prayer, especially prayer at the altar of incense, this process is lightning fast.

Worship is the flow of God's will, nature, and love from our hearts to His. It is a place of perfect intercession where prayers are answered, petitions are raised, and adoration and gratitude are expressed. More faith, confidence, assurance, and security are found at the altar of incense. The connectivity we all long for is fulfilled here, and it is here that our primary purpose becomes obvious: to be worshipers, representatives, intercessors, ambassadors, priests, Christians.

Just about every Christian has known the still, quiet voice of God in his or her heart. At the altar of incense, it is as if a trigger is pulled, and those words start to manifest in us. Remember, to enter the holy place, we manifest the obedience that is available to us because of the power of the blood and the ministry of the Holy Spirit. At the altar of incense, the manifestation increases. The written Word of God, the Bible, comes alive in us like never before.

Thus, our overwhelming gratitude produces even more worship and heartfelt prayer. Because we experience so much joy and freedom in the holy place, this is where we want to live.

The Good Life Gets Even Better

But there is somewhere else: the most holy place.

Most never go into the holy of holies. We are already complete in God, and the most holy place may not seem necessary. It is only entered by a few people. My guess is that fewer than 2 percent of us will ever be in the holy of holies this side of heaven.

At this point, you may feel you have enough. Most never leave the outer court, but hopefully you have. Most never find authentic security and rest, but hopefully you have. Most never know the flow of spiritual life flowing from their hearts to God, but hopefully you have. If so, you may have enough. You have more than most.

Now, read your Bible, faithfully participate in the body of Christ, serve with your whole heart, and do everything to the glory of God. Rest in the holiness that He has built into you, and enjoy being set apart for holy service in the way you relate to others. Be godly, and be contented. Rest here.

But if you cannot rest, let's go further—to the holy of holies.

Part Four

Staying in the Good Life

*In the outer court, we received and learned about
the operation of the gifts of the Spirit. In the holy
place, the gifts of the Spirit were used to bring Him
glory and honor. Now, in the most holy place, the
gifts of the Spirit are so much in us that we actually
become them.*

CHAPTER ELEVEN

Love: Approaching the Most Holy Place

When Christ entered the most holy place to make final atonement for our sins, He did so as the ultimate demonstration of love. In the same way, when we enter the most holy place, we follow His example of love by interceding for other people. We become representatives of Christ for our generation.

This is crucial. Don't miss this point: when we enter into the most holy place, we are there to glorify God, but we are also positioned to make petition for others who still need atonement. We can pray on their behalf before God as an act of ultimate love.

The importance of this idea will unfold as you read through this chapter. As we talk about what the priest did in the most holy place, we will see how we identify with Christ in turning our focus to living for the good of other people. We are priests, called to serve, and called to demonstrate the transforming love of God toward others. Love is central to experiencing the most holy place. God is love, and it is worth taking time here to meditate on the role of love in the pursuit of the good life.

Living for Others in the Most Holy Place

Entering the most holy place is an act of love, because the person who enters always does so on behalf of other people. When God was describing the priestly garments for Aaron, the first priest allowed to enter the most holy place, He instructed him to inscribe the names of the twelve sons (or tribes) of Israel on the garments. The Bible says:

> Aaron is to bear the names [of the sons of Israel]
> on his shoulders as a memorial before the LORD.
> —Exodus 28:12

Shoulders are a symbol of power, and Aaron was, in essence, taking the people before God with all his strength. In addition, the Bible says:

> Whenever Aaron enters the Holy Place, he will
> bear the names of the sons of Israel over his heart
> on the breastpiece of decision as a continuing
> memorial before the LORD.   —Exodus 28:29

The heart is a symbol of our passion. Aaron carried the people of God on his shoulders and on his heart into the holy of holies to make intercession for them. This was a type, or symbol, of what Jesus would do in reality.

As we follow Jesus' example and enter into the most holy place, we must be willing to carry others on our shoulders and in our hearts. We don't go in for ourselves—we carry people, and we ask God to bless them. In the holy of holies, our own needs diminish. We are overcome with satisfaction and long for that satisfaction to come to others. That is what is on God's heart, and we experience His heart.

Entering the most holy place—and pursuing the good life—is not about us. It is about others.

It is total self-denial.

It is real love—living for someone else's good.

In the next two chapters, we will look closely at what is inside the most holy place: the ark of the covenant, with the Ten Commandments and Aaron's rod stored inside. All those items have phenomenal significance for the pursuit of the good life in God.

But before we look at them, in order to really move us forward in pursuing the good life, let's keep talking about this issue of love.

Christians Bear the Mark of Love

I was raised on a farm in Indiana where love was demonstrated in practical ways. Mom and Dad would tell us how much they loved us, but it wasn't a gushy, effervescent emotional expression. Our culture considered that type of syrupy expression superficial and unreliable. The type of love I grew up with was the type that ensured that Mom and Dad would stay together all of their lives. It was the type of love that would guarantee that the poor kids in town received gifts at Christmas and that even the town drunk was employed on the days when he sobered up. Love manifested itself in solid, substantive ways.

We didn't ever lock our home, our cars, or our businesses. Many of the downtown businesses never locked their doors at night out of concern that someone might need something after hours. I remember my dad going into the Western Auto late one night, picking up some supplies, and leaving a note with the money on the cash register. He told the owner to keep the change.

Could this be a manifestation of Christian love? I think so. It is trust, safety, and respect for others—all attributes of selfless love.

As Christians, love is our marker. Jesus said:

> By this all men will know that you are my disciples, if you love one another.
> —John 13:35

The Greek word here has become a popular Christian word, *agape*, which is the perfect love of God that flows through the believer toward another. Demons cannot imitate this love, and false believers cannot fake it. This type of love is premeditated, observable, verifiable, and selfless. It marks us as Christians. Love is how people know that we believe in Jesus and have been changed by Him.

Love Is Not a Mystery

John's first epistle says a great deal about this incredible love that can work in the heart of every believer.

> This is the message you heard from the beginning: We should love one another. Do not be like Cain, who belonged to the evil one and murdered his brother. And why did he murder him? Because his own actions were evil and his brother's were righteous. Do not be surprised, my brothers, if the world hates you. We know that we have passed from death to life, because we love our brothers. Anyone who does not love remains in death. Anyone who hates his brother is a murderer, and you know that no murderer has eternal life in him. This is how we know what love is: Jesus Christ laid down his life for us. And we ought to lay down our lives for our brothers.
> —1 John 3:11–16

"We know what love is!" cries John. Biblically speaking, love is not a mystery. We know how to look for it, how to find it, and how to produce it because Jesus showed us all those things. Giving up your life—that is what real love looks like.

John continues his exhortation in the next two verses. Here he explains that godly love expresses itself through action:

> If anyone has material possessions and sees his
> brother in need but has no pity on him, how can
> the love of God be in him? Dear children, let us
> not love with words or tongue but with actions
> and in truth.
> —1 John 3:17–18

Words and feelings are not enough. If we do not love with actions—that is, with physical acts that people can observe—we are not loving in truth.

If love is an action, it can be verified. It is not just a feeling, which is why Jesus said:

> If you love me, you will obey what I command.
> —John 14:15

Jesus wants to see our love, just as we can see His. The Bible says:

> But God demonstrates his own love for us in this:
> While we were still sinners, Christ died for us.
> —Romans 5:8

He showed us what His love looked like. Now we can show Him, and others, the demonstration of our love.

Three Big Ideas About Love

The apostle Peter wrote:

> Now that you have purified yourselves by obey-
> ing the truth so that you have sincere love for
> your brothers, love one another deeply, from the
> heart.
> —1 Peter 1:22

Peter highlights three big ideas here. The first is *personal purity* and its relationship with sincere love. It is difficult to love others when our hearts are clouded with impurities. Our own sinfulness taints our view of others, causing us to be judgmental. Matthew 7:1–5 warns us against judging each other, comparing it to trying to take a speck of sawdust out of our brother's eye, all the while neglecting the plank that is in our own. Once we purify ourselves by ridding ourselves of sinfulness, innocence returns and we are able to love sincerely without judgment in our hearts.

Many people are afraid of the strong emotions associated with love because they confuse them with sexuality or immorality. But love and sex are not the same thing. We need to know the difference between the love of God working through us for the good of others and sexual attraction or temptation. God's love is pure, wholesome, and honorable, but only sexual in relationship to our spouses.

The second big idea that Peter develops is that *love can be sincere or deceptive*. Often people are dismayed because they have been nailed by a "sugar-coated dagger." I mean people who seem sweet and wonderful but are ready to do harm. They carry murderous weapons, covered in sugar, which is really another way of saying they have "insincere love."

> *Love and sex are not the same thing. We need to know the difference between the love of God working through us and sexual attraction or temptation.*

I saw this just a few weeks ago while working with a church whose pastor had been accused of immoral activity. Interestingly, some people on the pastor's staff were hoping the pastor was guilty, which he turned out to be. But before adequate evidence was known, between their comments about how they "loved him to death" they emphasized his many faults and weaknesses.

Actually, these associates were indeed loving their pastor to *his* death, rather than to their own. Of course, we know that loving someone to death is more than an empty euphemism—it is what Jesus did for us. He loved us enough to die for us. "I am the good shepherd," He said. "The good shepherd lays down his life for the sheep" (John 10:11).

First Corinthians 13:4–8 reveals the characteristics of authentic love. It says:

> Love is patient, love is kind. It does not envy, it does not boast, it is not proud. It is not rude, it is not self-seeking, it is not easily angered, it keeps no record of wrongs. Love does not delight in evil but rejoices with the truth. It always protects, always trusts, always hopes, always perseveres. Love never fails.

The third idea Peter mentions is that *love can be deep or shallow.* It is our choice. Love is not random but intentional. We decide how we will love and whom we will love. The level of love in our lives is up to us.

Not surprisingly, the most beautiful and lasting words on love come from Jesus. In His Sermon on the Mount, He highlighted how love is displayed not through mere words or feelings but through actions:

> Love your enemies, do good to those who hate you, bless those who curse you, pray for those who mistreat you. If someone strikes you on one cheek, turn to him the other also. If someone takes your cloak, do not stop him from taking your tunic. Give to everyone who asks you, and if anyone takes what belongs to you, do not demand it back. Do to others as you would have them do to you.

If you love those who love you, what credit is that to you? Even "sinners" love those who love them. And if you do good to those who are good to you, what credit is that to you? Even "sinners" do that. And if you lend to those from whom you expect repayment, what credit is that to you? Even "sinners" lend to "sinners," expecting to be repaid in full. But love your enemies, do good to them, and lend to them without expecting to get anything back. Then your reward will be great, and you will be sons of the Most High, because he is kind to the ungrateful and wicked. Be merciful, just as your Father is merciful.

—Luke 6:27–36

Love Means Living for Others

Many worry that love costs them too much because it can be rejected. No doubt, it takes faith to love. Jesus told us it would take selfless dedication, and it does.

It is sad to watch people today try to raise children or maintain a marriage when their purpose for children was their own satisfaction and their reason for marriage was their own pleasure. (Need an example? Check out this week's Hollywood tabloids.) Life doesn't work this way. Children are certainly good for us, but it's not because they are pieces of an appropriate life. It is because they teach us to live selflessly for another. In living for their good and dying to our own interests, we find life.

We cannot live for ourselves and find His purpose. We cannot live for ourselves and still love.

In the same way, marriage is a wonderful delight, but many teach that it takes a lot of work and is very difficult. I don't think so. Why? Because I did not get married just for me; I got married because I love Gayle. I decided on the day we got married that my marriage was not for me but for her. And in living for her, I found life myself. "Turn the other cheek." "Go the second mile." That is love—forgetting about your needs so that you can meet someone else's.

If our purpose for living is to help fulfill the Great Commission, then we are not living for ourselves. If our destiny is to find our own pleasure, fulfill our own dreams, and live our own lives, then we will never find His purpose, His destiny, and His dream for our lives. Nor will we experience real love. We cannot live for ourselves and find His purpose. We cannot live for ourselves and still love. Instead, we must die to ourselves and devote our lives to His purpose. In doing so, we love, and we truly live.

It seems to me that this generation or the next could complete the Great Commission. God is doing incredibly exciting work in the world, and this should motivate us to devote ourselves to His purpose.

But we can't be a part of it without authentic love. Since God is love (1 John 4:8, 16), everything He does is motivated by love for His people. Since we are His people, we must be motivated by love in order to participate positively in His plan. We must be intoxicated and motivated by the well-being of others. We need a fresh baptism of love. We find it in the most holy place.

CHAPTER TWELVE

The Good Rules: How God Instructs Us

We are in the most holy place, which the King James Version of the Bible calls the holy of holies. Here, the power and grace of God impact us with their greatest significance. Here, we will find the best good life we could ever imagine.

As I have said, the most holy place was such a significant room that the priest would only enter once a year. On the Day of Atonement, he would go past a curtain separating the holy place from the most holy place. Once inside, he would place blood on the mercy seat of the ark of the covenant in atonement for the sins of the people. That blood, we know now, was a symbol of the day when Jesus would place His blood on the actual mercy seat in heaven to atone for all of our sins.

When the priest performed this annual ritual, he did so with great fear, knowing that the intensity of the power of God might be overwhelming. It might even cost him his life. Encounters with angels and life-altering experiences with God were the norm in the most holy place.

Interestingly, while the records of the tabernacle are painstakingly detailed, there is one apparent omission: nowhere does the Old Testament explain how the priest went past the curtain into the most holy place. If you examine the illustration of the curtain on the facing page, you will notice that it had no split or seam, so we are not sure how he went from one room to the next.

Of course, he may have just pushed it aside or slipped under the bottom where the curtain touched the floor. But given the powerful, mysterious realities surrounding the tabernacle and the most holy place, and given the reverence with which the Jewish people treated these spaces, many have speculated that something else took place.

Some think that when the priest was standing at the altar of incense worshiping, he would suddenly find himself in the most holy place. I love this idea, because it stresses the importance of worshiping with purity, integrity, and security. When we do that, God removes the remaining barrier between Him and us, and He alone ushers us into His special sanctuary.

Another prevailing idea is that as the priest worshiped at the altar, the curtain would actually move behind him. Here again, this communicates how much God does to bring us into this sacred place. He makes room for us as we attempt to enter into the most holy place according to His established protocol.

Both of these options are a guess, of course. But it's not hard to believe that one of them might actually be true. I like these images more than the priest slipping himself in naturally. They reinforce the fact that we can do nothing on our own to enter the most holy place. God is the one who makes it possible.

The Most Holy Place Is Perfect

Some people would say that experiencing the most holy place is possible only in heaven. Only then, they argue, could we ever be

The Veil / The Entrance to Most Holy Place Living

in the fullness of God's plan. While we may always be removed by some degree from God while on Earth, I am not convinced that He can't bring us into fullness in the here and now. In fact, I think the account of the most holy place in Exodus is an example of the most perfect life we can live on Earth. This is where the good life really gets good.

The dimensions of the most holy place are a symbol of the highest perfection we could imagine on this earth. Its breadth and length and height were each an exact 15 feet: it was a cube, which is a perfect structure. Later, when Solomon built the temple, the most holy place was 30 feet by 30 feet by 30 feet—another cube (1 Kings 6:20).

Now, note a fascinating and crucial association: in Revelation 21, the Bible describes the New Jerusalem. It too is a perfect cube. Revelation 21:16 says:

> The city was laid out like a square, as long as it was wide. He measured the city with the rod and found it to be 12,000 stadia [that is, about 1,400 miles, or about 2,200 kilometers] in length, and as wide and high as it is long.

Just before this, John (the author of Revelation, to whom the visions were given) had seen the New Jerusalem for the first time. Revelation 21:1–4 says:

> Then I saw a new heaven and a new earth, for the first heaven and the first earth had passed away, and there was no longer any sea. I saw the Holy City, the new Jerusalem, coming down out of heaven from God, prepared as a bride beautifully dressed for her husband. And I heard a loud voice from the throne saying, "Now the dwelling of God is with men, and he will live with them. They will be his people, and God himself will be with them and be their God. He will wipe every tear from their eyes. There will be no more death or mourning or crying or pain, for the old order of things has passed away."

The New Jerusalem is the culmination of history. It is where creation is finally made perfect—no death, mourning, crying, or pain. Everyone is healed and made perfect, and all are united with their Creator for good.

I believe that we can develop a most holy place lifestyle where we see the culmination of our spiritual experiences on Earth. Again, the cube is a symbol of perfection because of its absoluteness of symmetry. Turn the cube and it is still the same—equally wide, high, and deep. The most holy place is perfection itself, and it symbolizes the ideal relationship we can have with God. There, we are really at home in Christ. There, we are living the good life in the most perfect way possible. I wonder if Paul was thinking of this when he wrote:

> How wide and long and high and deep is the love
> of Christ.
> —Ephesians 3:18

Paul was trying to adequately describe the perfect love of God that we can experience, and his language seems to drift toward the image of a perfect cube.

The Most Holy Place Is Holy

When people brought their offerings to the tabernacle, they were allowed into the outer court but not the holy place. As I have mentioned, 94 percent of the square footage of the tabernacle was dedicated to the outer court. The smallness of the holy place indicates its sacredness. The most holy place was only 2 percent of the whole, and only the high priest was permitted into this sacred place of worship—and even he could enter but once a year and only after special preparation. These same stipulations applied later when Solomon built the temple.

Wherever God dwells on Earth, that place becomes unspeakably sacred. God wanted this lesson communicated to the people, and it is important that we understand it as well. There cannot be acceptable worship or true fellowship without a reverent recognition of God's sacredness. That's why protocol is so crucial: sacrifice at the bronze altar, water and Holy Spirit baptism at the bronze basin, taking on Christ's identity and living a life of active obedience, walking in the pure light of the lamp stand, praying and worshiping at the altar of incense—all of this has to happen before entering the most holy place.

The Most Holy Place Is God's Residence

The most holy place is perfect, it is holy, and finally, within the tabernacle, it is where God dwelt. Think about this: the tabernacle in the wilderness was God's first dwelling place on Earth. He had visited with and dealt with mankind before, but He hadn't established a residence among them. He had walked with Adam and Eve in Eden, He had spoken to the patriarchs, He had visited Abraham, He had become friends with Moses, but He hadn't moved into any location on Earth. Now, however, with the tabernacle, God wanted His people to understand that He was very present with them. It was as if He was moving into their neighborhood.

God is everywhere. But He can make His real presence available wherever He chooses.

I believe that from the tabernacle on, God has established dwelling places for Himself to live among or through His people on Earth. Yes, God is everywhere. But He can make His presence manifest wherever He chooses. After God lived in the most holy place of the tabernacle, He resided in the most holy place in Solomon's temple. Then He chose to make the church His very body and to make us His very temples. Ephesians 2:21–22 says we are "a holy temple...built together to become a dwelling in which God lives by his Spirit." We are God's place of residence on Earth—"For we are the temple of the living God. As God has said: 'I will live with them and walk among them, and I will be their God, and they will be my people'" (2 Cor. 6:16)—and will continue to be until the consummation of history.

Making a Way Through the Curtain

When Jesus died on the cross, the seamless curtain between the holy place and the most holy place was torn in two. Matthew 27:50–51 says:

> And when Jesus had cried out again in a loud voice, he gave up his spirit. At that moment the curtain of the temple was torn in two from top to bottom. The earth shook and the rocks split.

Remember, this curtain separated the holy place—where the priest prayed and gave thanks on behalf of the people—from the most holy place, which was God's dwelling place. The curtain stood for the solemn truth that because humans were sinful, they could not freely approach God. Access to the most holy place was severely restricted. The high priest could enter only one day each year to represent the people, and then only if he brought with him the blood of an atoning sacrifice. The way for all God's people to enter freely into His presence had not yet been provided.

So when Jesus died, the tearing of the curtain meant that God had removed the barrier. Look at the description of this truth in Hebrews 10:19–27, which includes an exhortation for us to live powerful, godly lives:

> Therefore, brothers, since we have confidence to enter the Most Holy Place by the blood of Jesus, by a new and living way opened for us through the

curtain, that is, his body, and since we have a great priest over the house of God, let us draw near to God with a sincere heart in full assurance of faith, having our hearts sprinkled to cleanse us from a guilty conscience and having our bodies washed with pure water. Let us hold unswervingly to the hope we profess, for he who promised is faithful. And let us consider how we may spur one another on toward love and good deeds. Let us not give up meeting together, as some are in the habit of doing, but let us encourage one another—and all the more as you see the Day approaching. If we deliberately keep on sinning after we have received the knowledge of the truth, no sacrifice for sins is left, but only a fearful expectation of judgment and of raging fire that will consume the enemies of God.

The torn curtain makes it possible for every one of us to be filled with the abiding Holy Spirit and actually become the dwelling place of God on Earth. Now we are all able to experience the presence and power of God in a personal, dynamic way.

As a result of Christ's sacrifice, God doesn't just dwell in the temple. He lives in us. We are the temple. We are the most holy place, and the ark of the covenant is within us.

Ingredients for the Good Life

The ark of the covenant, shown on the facing page, was kept in the most holy place. The ark contained the Ten Commandments (Deut. 10:1–2), a pot of manna (Exod. 16:32–34), and Aaron's rod that budded (Num. 17:10–11; Heb. 9:4). I'll explain the first item here and the next two in the next chapter.

The Ark of the Covenant / God's Presence

The fact that the Ten Commandments are in the ark shows us the importance of the law. Obedience to the law does not save us, of course, nor does it make us like God. But obedience to specific commands does provide the protection and guidance each of us needs in order to manifest successfully the godly righteousness Christ places in us.

In Hebrews 10, where the Bible explains the opportunities available to us because of the torn curtain, there are strong exhortations about obedience. Verses 28–31 say:

> Anyone who rejected the law of Moses died without mercy on the testimony of two or three witnesses. How much more severely do you think a man deserves to be punished who has trampled the Son of God under foot, who has treated as an unholy thing the blood of the covenant that

sanctified him, and who has insulted the Spirit of grace? For we know him who said, "It is mine to avenge; I will repay," and again, "The Lord will judge his people." It is a dreadful thing to fall into the hands of the living God.

Interestingly, the explanation about the curtain in the most holy place and the importance of our obedience comes after we are reminded, "I will put my laws in their hearts, and I will write them on their minds" (v. 16). This is why as we study the Bible, the Word bears witness in our hearts and minds. We draw not failure and condemnation from God's law, but life and power.

> *In heeding New Testament warnings about the weakness of the law to create righteousness, we have unwisely discarded the value of the law to protect us.*

The Ten Commandments represent the need for every person to have a "core," a set of values at the center of their life. These values don't change, are not moved, and stand firm in the midst of shifting situations and stormy weather. Having a core protects us, our families, and our future.

So the law is a protective barrier around my life. It provides incredible moral strength. That's why I love the laws of God. I enjoy them. I embrace them and thank God for them. In one of David's psalms, he communicated the life we can draw from embracing God's standards. I encourage you to stop here and read Psalm 119, but here is a sampling of the joy David found in God's law:

> Blessed are they whose ways are blameless, who walk according to the law of the LORD.
>
> —Psalm 119:1

Blessed are they who keep his statutes and seek him with all their heart.
—Psalm 119:2

I will praise you with an upright heart as I learn your righteous laws.
—Psalm 119:7

I rejoice in following your statutes as one rejoices in great riches.
—Psalm 119:14

I delight in your decrees; I will not neglect your word.
—Psalm 119:16

Open my eyes that I may see wonderful things in your law.
—Psalm 119:18

Your statutes are my delight; they are my counselors.
—Psalm 119:24

I am a strong advocate of the biblical truth of salvation by grace through faith. But in heeding New Testament warnings about the weakness of the law to create righteousness, we have unwisely discarded the value of the law to protect us. As a result, many Christians believe they have a position of righteousness because of their faith in the cross, but they have no evidence of that faith in their lives. They might be Christians (or think they are Christians), but because they are not abiding by God's law, they are without protection.

I know we don't want to think like this. But the law of God gives us a core, protects us, and opens the door for us to live a better life. If we decide not to commit adultery, our odds of having a great marriage are much better. If we decide not to lie, the odds are that we will have an honorable reputation. If we decide to honor our father and mother, our likelihood of having a healthy relationship with our parents is much better. If we choose to obey the laws of the land, the chances of us having a criminal record are greatly reduced.

This is not hard to understand. Standards protect our lives.

What About All the Other Commandments?

When I teach on embracing the statutes of God, I regularly have people ask me how to sort out the Old Testament laws that apply to us today. It is pretty clear that all of the Ten Commandments are applicable for us today. But we don't practice so many other things in the Bible. How do we choose?

I believe that the moral, behavioral, and spiritual principles in the Bible are timeless. All the precepts that teach us about the nature of God apply to us today. The scriptures that apply to a specific historic situation don't necessarily apply; still, they may teach us some principles about godly living. Even some of the seemingly arcane ritual instructions can be appreciated for the way they point to New Testament life.

> *I believe that the moral, behavioral, and spiritual principles in the Bible are timeless. All the precepts that teach us about the nature of God apply to us today.*

The main idea to remember when reading the Old Testament is that we are unable to obtain righteousness through obedience to the law. Righteousness only comes from faith in Christ. The law, though, protects our lives from failure, and, of course, it also helps us manifest obedience.

We can live safer, more honorable lives if, like David, we can claim, "I have hidden your word in my heart, that I might not sin against you" (Ps. 119:11).

Yes, godly living is empowered only by God, but it is not hard. And the Ten Commandments in the ark of the covenant are there to remind us that God does have an opinion, He is the Creator of the universe, and He knows how our lives should be ordered.

CHAPTER THIRTEEN

The Good Life: How to Find the Best Possible Life

Inside the most holy place is the ark of the covenant, which contains several items—shown on page 160—that indicate how to live the best possible life here on Earth. In the last chapter, we looked at the Ten Commandments, which provide the core of our lives. Without standards, we don't know how to do the right things. But with principles, precepts, and the law of God protecting our lives every day, we can live in joy and peace.

By itself, the law is insufficient. We have to abide by the law in the context of life—budding, flowing, effervescent life. That is why Aaron's rod that budded is also found in the ark of the covenant.

Numbers 16 tells the story of a rebellion led by a Levite named Korah. Along with some other leaders, including two hundred fifty Israelite council members, this group "became insolent and rose up against Moses" (vv. 1–2). The issue? They wanted equality before God along with Moses and Aaron, who were God's appointed community leaders. "You have gone too far!" they complained. "The whole community is holy, every one of them,

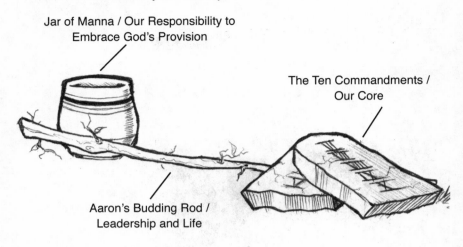

Jar of Manna / Our Responsibility to
Embrace God's Provision

The Ten Commandments /
Our Core

Aaron's Budding Rod /
Leadership and Life

Items Inside the Ark of the Covenant

and the LORD is with them. Why then do you set yourselves above the LORD's assembly?" (v. 3).

Numbers 16 is worth a close reading because it gives the account of God defending His choice of Moses and Aaron. The story demonstrates God's desire to have specific people perform specific roles. Often, average people—that is, people who may be good leaders but who have not been especially chosen by God for the task they *wish* they were chosen for—have a hard time living with the way God works. The fact is, God chooses whomever He chooses, and the only appropriate response is to accept that. In Korah's rebellion, too many people could not see past their own desires, and fourteen thousand people died as a result.

But the story does not end there. In the next chapter of Numbers, Moses asks for the staff of each of the leaders of the twelve tribes of Israel. Each leader put their name on their staff, and Aaron's name was put on the staff representing the tribe of Levi. The purpose? God wanted to show once and for all that He had a specific leader chosen for all of Israel. He had them put their staffs inside the tent of the testimony and leave them there overnight. "The staff belonging to the man I choose will sprout," God said to Moses, "and I will rid myself of this constant grumbling against you by the Israelites" (Num. 17:5).

The next morning, when Moses entered the tent to retrieve the staffs, he saw a remarkable sight: "Aaron's staff, which represented the house of Levi, had not only sprouted but had budded, blossomed and produced almonds" (v. 8). God told Moses to leave Aaron's staff in front of the tent as a sign to anyone with further thoughts of rebelling against God and His chosen leaders. God had made His decision about who would lead Israel. No further discussion would be had.

Hebrews 9:4 tells us that Aaron's rod that budded was later placed in the ark of the covenant along with the tablets of the Ten Commandments and a jar of manna. The significance of the rod is twofold:

1. It tells us that God's delegated authority must be respected.

2. It tells us that God identifies leaders with signs of life.

Submission Leads to Life

Let's look at a couple of verses that highlight how God wants us to see our leaders.

> Remember your leaders, who spoke the word of God to you. Consider the outcome of their way of life and imitate their faith.
> —Hebrews 13:7

Remembering leaders is a process and a practice. We don't just acknowledge them absently, and we don't just put up with them. Rather, we "consider" their lives. We investigate. We look closely. We discern *why* God has chosen them—what qualities and attributes does God see in them? Then we imitate them. We act like them and try to add their characteristics to our lives.

Romans 13:1–5 likewise highlights the importance of those in authority over us. It says:

> Everyone must submit himself to the governing authorities, for there is no authority except that which God has established. The authorities that exist have been established by God. Consequently, he who rebels against the authority is rebelling against what God has instituted, and those who do so will bring judgment on themselves. For rulers hold no terror for those who do right, but for those who do wrong. Do you want to be free from fear of the one in authority? Then do what is right and he will commend you. For he is God's servant to do you good. But if you do wrong, be afraid, for he does not bear the sword for nothing. He is God's servant, an agent of wrath to bring punishment on the wrongdoer. Therefore, it is necessary to submit to the authorities, not only because of possible punishment but also because of conscience.

Rebellion against God's delegated authorities is rebellion against God's order. If we can grasp this, then it is not hard to understand why Aaron's rod is included at the heart of the most holy place. The rod addresses the issue of rebellion, which is a high-minded worldview that we can judge virtually everyone and everything. The rod tells us to humble ourselves and submit to God, to others, and to His plan. It tells us to become people who obey the rules. The truth is that submitting to God's established leadership is a major part of what it means to live the most perfect life in the most holy place.

First Timothy 2:1–4 gives us a strong exhortation about this subject. Here Paul writes to his young disciple Timothy and says:

> I urge, then, first of all, that requests, prayers, intercession and thanksgiving be made for everyone—for kings and all those in authority, that we may live peaceful and quiet lives in all godliness and holiness. This is good, and pleases God our Savior, who wants all men to be saved and to come to a knowledge of the truth.

In these verses, Paul lists three outcomes of treating leadership with prayerful respect:

1. Acknowledging and praying for our leaders produce lives of peace and quiet. Praying and thanking God for our leaders are keys to being godly and holy.

2. Acknowledging and praying for our leaders please God.

3. Acknowledging and praying for leaders seem to be necessary to helping others come to Christ.

Over the years, I have found that people have a hard time following the advice of these verses for a very simple reason: they do not know who their leaders are. Many Christians are perfectly happy to pray for those in authority, but they have never taken the time to identify their leaders and their leaders' responsibilities.

I suggest making a list of those in authority over you. Start with your family (i.e., parents), then list leaders in your church, workplace, and city, state, and national government. Do this, and you will know whom God has appointed over you, and you will know how to fulfill 1 Timothy 2:1–4.

By and large, this is not difficult. Think broadly, and you will see that it is very easy to understand how leadership works in our lives and how little we have to wrestle with it.

I know you are thinking about the times when God's delegated authorities have abused their authority and hurt people. What should we do then?

Our responsibility is to obey the Bible first, so if any delegated authority orders you to do something contrary to the Word of God, then obey the Bible and disobey the delegated authority. Most of the time, however, we have to deal with the ambiguity of apparently subjective commands given by designated authorities. Most of the time, we should just obey even if it does not feel right. If we do, we will find that we are able to live a peaceful and quiet life in all godliness and holiness.

So, as you see, it is not that hard. I jokingly tell people that if they will obey God's Word, they won't need so many miracles. If our lives are empowered and protected by God's Word, we won't need God to overcome problems we have created through our rebellion, disobedience, and arrogance.

On October 15, 2005, the National Socialist Movement was going to march through a small section of Toledo, Ohio, to demonstrate against the black gangs that had reportedly been harassing white residents. This incensed black residents so much that a group of them turned violent, throwing baseball-sized rocks at police, vandalizing vehicles and stores, and setting fire to a bar in their neighborhood. It took one hundred fifty police officers in helicopters, on horseback, and on foot to chase the bands of youths throughout the afternoon. Officers wearing gas masks fired tear gas canisters and flash-bang devices designed to stun suspects, only to see the groups reappear nearby and resume throwing rocks and bottles.

All of this could have been avoided. The mayor, in anticipation of the tension caused by the planned march, appealed to residents to ignore it. They didn't, and many are suffering because of it.

The National Socialist Movement never actually marched. Their march was canceled by the city.

Life does not have to be nearly as bad as we make it for one another. The vast majority of suffering that happens on Earth is imposed on people by other people. The AIDS pandemic is primarily the result of promiscuity and rape; it could end within this generation by compliance to the biblical standard of sexual activity within heterosexual monogamous marriage. When the hurricanes hit the southern coast of the United States in the summer of 2005, New Orleans suffered a natural disaster, but the suffering of the people of New Orleans would not have been compounded in the days that followed if more citizens had been obedient to the government officials and evacuated the city.

The point: open the ark of the covenant. Embrace the Ten Commandments and have a solid inner core that will protect your life. Take up Aaron's budded rod and reject your rebellion. Flow in life. And remember, love is what leads you into the most holy place. Before you get caught up in legalism or judgment, remember: it is all about love. The more you love God, the more you will love His law and His leaders. The more you love others, the more you will rejoice with those who embrace God's laws, and the more you will intercede for those who don't. Love leads to life. Love, and you will be living a key component of the good life.

The Life of God Himself

Aaron's rod is also a reminder of the power of life. His rod was not just filled with buds, but it was actually sprouting blossoms and almonds. The other staffs were just as they had been—dead. God designated His chosen authority with an act of life. Aaron's rod represents the life of God Himself.

The Bible opens with God creating an environment for life as well as life itself. The Bible closes with the river of life and the tree of life in Revelation 22. The Bible is the book of life. Jesus is the bread of life. The Holy Spirit is living water, which is the basic nutrient of life. Life is key.

Life (and Death) in the Garden

The easiest way I know of to grasp the depth of this idea is to look at the story of Adam and Eve in the Garden of Eden. I believe in a literal Adam and Eve and a literal garden. But I also think that Genesis, like so many Old Testament accounts, is saturated with New Testament applications.

> *The God of Abraham, Isaac, and Jacob is spirit, and He will not be related to on a purely intellectual level.*

When Eve had to choose between the tree of life and the tree of the knowledge of good and evil, she faced the struggle that every person who wants to please God faces: should we know God in the simplicity and innocence of the life that He offers us, or should we try to know Him based on information (knowledge) about good things and evil things? If we try to relate to God based on the facts that we know about good and evil, we may derive some satisfaction from living good lives, but in our hearts, we will die.

This is how the scribes and Pharisees of Jesus' day missed the point, and why every other religion and many Christians miss living the good life. The God of Abraham, Isaac, and Jacob is spirit, and He will not be related to on a purely intellectual level. He is life itself. He must be ingested. He must be known, not just known about. As Jesus told the Jewish leaders of His day:

> You diligently study the Scriptures because you
> think that by them you possess eternal life. These
> are the Scriptures that testify about me, yet you
> refuse to come to me to have life.
> —John 5:39

To know about God, even according to the Scriptures, is woefully inadequate. We have to receive life from the Author of life.

Many Christians have assented to the truth intellectually, and they enjoy the security of that truth. They are like Eve in Genesis 3:6–7, where she found that consuming the knowledge of good and evil in order to be like God was good for food (internally satisfying), pleasing to the eye (looked good), and desirable for gaining wisdom (depth of insight). She and her husband had their eyes opened (they realized things they had not understood before) as they grew in their knowledge of good and evil. These are characteristics that are all too common among Christians and Christian leaders. They have a form of godliness that is, in fact, impressive, but too often they deny the power of God—or are at least uncomfortable with it.

Adam and Eve inadvertently realized they were naked and needed to cover up. *Nakedness* in the Genesis account is like the idea of *childlikeness* in Jesus' teaching. Jesus admonished people to embrace innocence, not cover it up. He said:

> Whoever humbles himself like this child is the
> greatest in the kingdom of heaven.
> —Matthew 18:4

He emphasized this idea more strongly when He said:

> I tell you the truth, anyone who will not receive
> the kingdom of God like a little child will never
> enter it.
> —Mark 10:15

When Adam and Eve appropriated the knowledge of good and evil, they began to believe that their innocence was inadequate.

They wanted knowledge in order to be "like God," but they missed the point—God does possess all knowledge, but He also possesses all innocence, all purity, all *life*. God is the great Both/ And. Knowledge *and* Innocence. Wisdom *and* Joy. He is life, and life is more than living by what you know with your mind.

Innocence is the conduit for God's Spirit in our lives, and the flow of His Spirit gives us a childlike delight that both gives us life and projects life onto everyone around us. New Testament believers must drink the water of life, or else we will feel the need to cover our shamefulness just as Adam and Eve did. Those who ingest the knowledge of good and evil in order to be like God cover up, displace responsibility, and become adept at blame and judgment. Worse, they find themselves blocked from the garden, held back from the tree of life. They may know a great deal about God, and certainly understand good and evil. They may have some religious satisfaction and be able to talk a lot about God's standards, but they lack intimacy, power, and the fruitful evidence of connectivity.

Life is better than death. Grasp Aaron's rod that budded, and live the life that is truly life.

Manna Appeared on the Desert Floor, Not in Their Mouths

In Exodus 16:32, God instructed Moses, "Take an omer of manna and keep it for the generations to come, so they can see the bread I gave you to eat in the desert when I brought you out of Egypt." This jar of manna was included in the ark of the covenant for two reasons. First, manna is clearly a symbol of God's sovereign provision. But less obviously, manna is also a reminder of personal responsibility.

As I explained in an earlier chapter, there were rules and regulations regarding manna. Most importantly, the Israelites had to go out and actually gather it six days of the week. On Friday, they were to gather a double portion so they would have food to eat on Saturday, when no manna would appear. God provided for them sovereignly, but the manna appeared on the floor of the desert, not in their mouths! So the pot of manna in the ark reveals the balance God established between the use of His sovereign power and our own responsibility to receive His provision.

In this way, the tabernacle provides a solution to a theological paradox that has been around for centuries and is still with us today: do we have free will, or does God decide the outcome of our lives?

The outer court and its furniture emphasize that part of our relationship with God that is based on human free will. In the outer court, we are encouraged to seek God, respond to His wooing, and live a life of obedience. In the outer court, we learn about our responsibility to respond to what God has made available to us.

The Scriptures undeniably show that we should be careful about personal responsibility. And the inclusion of the manna in the ark emphasizes that responsibility—God will provide, but we have to gather and care for that provision.

If the outer court emphasizes personal responsibility, the holy place emphasizes God's sovereign plan and will for our lives. As you will recall, the holy place is a place of total security and confidence in God's plan for our lives. In the holy place, we find the depth of

> *The pot of manna in the ark reveals the balance God established between the use of His sovereign power and our own responsibility to receive His provision.*

our inheritance in Christ and the security of His work and His nature, and we learn to rest. In the holy place, His sovereignty comes alive in us. The holy place illuminates the way God's grace and power set us apart and assure us of His determination to complete the work that He has begun in our lives.

By now, you can see what we have been coming to in our journey through the tabernacle. We have accepted our responsibility to respond to God's call on our lives and to find our primary purpose. We have learned to accept His sacrifice, be baptized, take on Christ's identity, and pursue holiness. We have also learned that God's love for us is absolute and that we can have total confidence in Him. God wants to accomplish His will through us, and we can be sure that He will do so as we consume the bread of life, live in His light and worship, and pray at the altar of incense.

Now, with the ark of the covenant inside the most holy place, everything comes together. God is sovereign, and we are responsible to fulfill His plan. He is sovereign. We are responsible. Both/ and. In the most holy place, the two paradigms are inseparable, and they come together beautifully in our hearts and lives.

The most holy place is the place that offers the good life. It's incredible. Here, we see that we need:

1. Standards that form our core

2. Life that overcomes death, especially the death that comes from rebellion

3. Manna that illustrates God's sovereign provision for His people, *and* the reality that His people had to get up and take what had been given according to God's instructions

These three ideas that are found in the ark of the covenant are covered in the redemptive blood of Christ, which is found on the mercy seat of God. Here, we have the abiding presence of God. Here, we are the fullness of the temple of the Holy Spirit. God's Word is alive. Our role is defined. Our destiny is secure. We know our purpose, and we know how to live the good life.

CHAPTER FOURTEEN

Truly Good: The Life You Are Meant to Live

Y ou are not an accident. Before the creation of the world, God decided that you would be born in this generation. He chose your family, the place where you would be born, and the situation surrounding your birth. He carefully designed you so that you would be able to make a contribution to the master plan He has for His creation. He designed you to be His friend, His cola-borer, His ambassador. And He intends for you to spend eternity with Him.

You were not designed to fail. You were not created to be end-lessly frustrated. God wants you to do some things, and He wants you to do those things well.

God wants you to be wholly His, to be completely enveloped in His life and love. But He also wants you to be able to argue a point, to communicate clearly, and to work to make life better for others.

Everything in the natural and in daily life as we see it around us and in the media suggests that you could never be what God wants you to be. You should be arrogant, high-minded, unprincipled, shallow, and loveless. But God's plan for you trumps all of that. You might feel as if you are doomed to that kind of life, but don't believe it. It's a lie. God loves you. He wants you to have a great life. He wants you to be someone others want to be around. He wants to use you for His purposes from now until the day you get to go home to Him.

In order to ensure that you can understand His purpose and plan for your life, He gave the picture of the tabernacle. Through looking at it and its contents, you can know His protocol for meeting Him and abiding in Him. The tabernacle is a picture of the most perfect life we can have in God.

Your relationship with God is so important that He has preserved this picture over thousands of years so you can have clear information about how to know Him. Just as a child needs to grow in his understanding of relationships—parents and siblings, friends and colleagues—so he can mature and have a wise and successful life, so God wants you to grow in relationship with Him so you can have the life He designed for you.

God wants this for all of us, which is why He desires to take us into His most holy place. There, we learn about the core beliefs that protect us. There, we learn about the life of God that annihilates our rebellious intentions. There, we learn to balance an appreciation for God's sovereignty with our personal responsibilities. These principles, covered in the blood of the mercy seat and surrounded by the angels, place us in God's presence with such power and assurance that we can live the good life—for good.

Finding Competence in the Most Holy Place

Bible scholars have long highlighted the most holy place as a space in which to meet with God in a special, powerful way. No doubt this is true. But I think it begs a question: Why would God want to meet with us? For love? Yes. And for fellowship, for revealing His purposes, and more. All of that is essential, and we have been learning about those issues all along our journey through the tabernacle.

But there is something else. Competence. The good life in its best, most able form. Nothing highlights competence like the most holy place.

Really? "Competence"? That's what all this is about?

What I want you to understand is that the most holy place is about being solid. It is about stability. It is about having depth, nuance, flexibility, and stature. The most holy place is a picture of the Christian life at its most successful. Full faith. Real confidence. Trust. Security. It is not super-spiritual. It is not hokey. It is competent.

Some Bible scholars might argue that the most holy place represents an encounter with God so dynamic and powerful that there is nothing like it out-side of heaven, and there-fore nothing else for us to appreciate about this place. Some feel that at this point God has already opened up His habitation to us and showed us how to dwell with Him. And that much is true. He has turned His written Word into creative words within us, making it

> *The most holy place is a picture of the Christian life at its most successful....It is not super-spiritual. It is not hokey. It is competent.*

so in our lives. He has met with us in such a special way that our prayers are powerfully answered by Him. After this, *surely*, the only remaining step can be the totally unveiled meeting with God that will occur in heaven.

Maybe so. But I'm not convinced. I think there is something else for us to grasp about this place. I think in the most holy place, we come to a place of responsibility *and* friendship, peace *and* fear. I think we come to a place of absolute love and divine terror. And I think this place turns us into capable people. Quality humans. Dependable. Trustworthy. Lasting. The most holy place makes our lives to be incredibly proficient. It brings everything we have experienced to fullness as we live for Him day after day.

The most holy place means competence. It makes us "good Christian people." It means that we really know how to live, and we do it.

From Having Gifts to Being a Gift

In the outer court, we received and learned about the operation of the gifts of the Spirit. There we needed them to operate for our survival, strengthening, and edification. There the gifts assisted in the continual transformation of our lives. In the holy place, the gifts of the Spirit were used to bring Him glory and honor. They were used to infuse our lives with His life and to focus us on His purposes and His calling during our generation. They flowed naturally and beautifully and did the work of the kingdom.

Now, in the most holy place, the gifts of the Spirit are so much in us that we actually become them. Here's what I mean. Paul writes:

> To one there is given through the Spirit the message of wisdom, to another the message of knowledge by means of the same Spirit, to another faith by the same Spirit, to another gifts of healing by that one Spirit, to another miraculous powers, to another prophecy, to another distinguishing between spirits, to another speaking in different kinds of tongues, and to still another the interpretation of tongues. All these are the work of one and the same Spirit, and he gives them to each one, just as he determines.
> —1 Corinthians 12:8–11

For centuries, Christians have read this passage and prayed that God would impart these gifts into them. And He freely does so according to His will. Usually, however, we understand these gifts to work in particular moments. In a prayer service or church meeting, for example, a believer will experience a message of wisdom and speak that message out to the church, to a smaller group of people, or to an individual person. Likewise, a believer may suddenly receive a word of knowledge and speak that word to the person for whom it is intended. That is the way we normally understand these gifts to operate in us, and that way has been a blessing to the church for ages.

But the most holy place brings a subtle and important alteration. Here, rather than having occasional, momentary experiences of wisdom, we become wisdom. Wisdom inhabits us. Rather than enjoying the delight of faith working in us from time to time, we are people of faith—rock-solid, unshakable faith. Faith becomes our entire worldview. It exists at the core of our beings. Rather than having an occasional message of knowledge, our very lives— day in, day out—become messages of knowledge. We can gain, comprehend, and correctly appropriate information. Instead of being able to prophesy from time to time, our lives will prophesy to the world that God is doing great things in the earth. We live the gifts. We are the gifts.

In no way do I mean to diminish the significance of the manifestation of singular gifts in people during worship services or prayer times. The gifts of the Spirit will continue to operate just as Paul explained to the Corinthians. But the most holy place is about God building everything into our hearts in such a way that we no longer simply host the gifts of the Holy Spirit. Now, the gifts of the Holy Spirit are so much in us that they actually become the core of our being.

Live for God, and He will show you how to live. He will use your life as a message of wisdom. The good life means that God's work in your life positively impacts normal situations. The way you respond to the daily news will communicate true knowledge. The way you respond to television will communicate faith. The way you respond to sexuality will communicate healing. God will integrate power into your life. You will be known as a person with substance, a person with an unshakable core.

What is true for the gifts of the Spirit is also true for the fruit of the Spirit. As I mentioned in chapter eight, Galatians 5:22–23 says:

> But the fruit of the Spirit is love, joy, peace, patience, kindness, goodness, faithfulness, gentleness and self-control. Against such things there is no law.

> *It's not enough to just enjoy the things of God. We instead have to become competent people whose lives are the things of God.*

In the most holy place, these characteristics are naturally part of your life. You won't have love for some and hatred for others. You won't feel joy at times and despair other times. In the most holy place, these traits burst forth from your life. You are kind. You are faithful. You are patient. You can control yourself. That's most holy place living.

Why is this so important? Because it's not enough to just *enjoy* the things of God. We instead have to become competent people whose lives *are* the things of God. The gifts and fruit of the Spirit are no longer guests in us. They are our personalities. They are our entire framework. They are the formative characteristics of our lives. We don't strive for them as attributes; they are simply part of who we are.

Whatever Your Hand Finds To Do

Now we're there. With these character qualities imbedded in our hearts and showing up in our daily lives, we can live in the fullness of God's perfect plan by faithfully doing what God places before us to do each day.

Clearly, this issue gets at one of the pressing issues for Christians today: calling. What do you think you are called to be? Some say, "I'm called to be a police officer." Others say, "I'm called to be a professor." But what do they do between the time they are "called" and the time in which they are actually doing those things? And what do they do if it takes years—and *years*—to reach those goals, or if something happens in life that impedes their "calling"? Does that mean they are wasting time or are outside of God's plan?

I don't think our calling is necessarily defined by what we do for a living. I think our lives are directed by His sovereign will as we competently execute the tasks He lays before us. We need to study, we need to learn, we need to be wise. And we need to do joyfully whatever is presented before us today.

Ecclesiastes 9:10 says:

> Whatever your hand finds to do, do it with all your might, for in the grave, where you are going, there is neither working nor planning nor knowledge nor wisdom.

With this verse, Solomon was saying that because life is precious and time is short, the time to be competent is *now*. Do what is in front of you. Don't run from task to task. Don't rush from calling to calling. Don't chase God's will all your life. It is right in front of you. Embrace what you see.

Many of you know the story of the talents that Jesus told His followers (Matt. 25:14–30). A recap: A rich man who is about to go on a journey hands out "talents," or sums of money worth over a thousand dollars each, to three of his servants. He gives five talents to one man, two talents to another man, and one talent to another. When the master returns from his trip, he finds that the servant with five talents had earned five more and the servant with two had earned two more, but the servant with one talent had buried it for safekeeping. Of course, the master rewards the first two servants but punishes the last. "For everyone who has will be given more," Jesus says, "and he will have an abundance. Whoever does not have, even what he has will be taken from him" (v. 29).

> *I don't think our calling is necessarily defined by what we do for a living. I think our lives are directed by His sovereign will as we competently execute the tasks He lays before us.*

Jesus told this parable so that we could decide what kind of servant we want to be. He is giving us the choice. Either we can take what He has given us—whether one, two, or ten talents; whether a fancy house or an apartment; whether a position of authority or a position of service—and make it grow for Him, or we can bury His gifts. We know what He wants. He wants us to do whatever our hand finds to do every day, and do it well. He wants us to be competent. He wants us to live in the most holy place.

God wants to give you the best ideas. He wants you to love selflessly. He wants you to have faith and hope and to share it intelligently and warmly with others. You are the salt of the earth. You are the light of the world. He wants you so He can use you, and He knows how to use you perfectly. He wants your mind, your possessions, your looks. Every piece of you is His, and He wants to use every piece for His purposes.

The Available Life

My wife, Gayle, and I have been married for twenty-seven years. When I proposed to Gayle, I explained to her everything I knew about God's call on my life. Then I asked her if she wanted to be part of that call. She said yes. Then I asked her to marry me, and she said yes again.

When she married me, she didn't simply marry Ted-Haggard-from-a-farm-in-Indiana. She married a calling. Because of that calling, we have known what we are committed to from day one. We have never valued houses, cars, or vacations. We have never valued recognition or size of ministry. Neither of us ever thought we would enjoy any creature comforts. Even though we enjoy many of the things this world has to offer, we never thought they would come our way.

You see, most holy place living has transformed us. We understand that if bad things happen to us, it's normal. That's how things tend to go on Earth. But if good things happen to us, it is a gift from God. As a result, we do not get bitter about things that are hard, and we are always grateful about things that are good.

Because of this worldview, if Gayle and I are ever able to go on a nice vacation or enjoy a meal at a fine restaurant, we consider it a gift. Giving media interviews and meeting with decision makers to discuss big ideas—those are gifts, not expectations. The opportunity to write a book like this is a gift, too. We do not demand or expect any of this, but we are available to do whatever God asks of us.

Right now, I serve as the president of the National Association of Evangelicals. But because I am a most holy place man, I serve there not because I deserve it, but because my life is available. I serve as president just as I would joyfully serve as usher at one of our events. I am called to serve. The difference between the presidency and ushering or cleaning up after a meeting is indistinguishable to me.

In this role, I am honored to meet with President George Bush, Prime Minister Tony Blair, and Prime Minister Ariel Sharon in order to work on issues. But I don't assume that they need me. Answering their questions and helping work on projects for them are a gift. I'm grateful. I try to be as helpful as possible, knowing that life may take a turn and that I may never meet with another significant decision maker in my lifetime. That too is OK. I would be just as happy helping a single mom balance her budget as I am discussing forgiving African debt with Tony Blair and debating the economic consequences of such a move. To me, those projects have equal value.

I am available to God. If God wants me working on African economies, Middle Eastern security, right-to-life issues in America, or a wayward teenage boy, I am available.

Maybe it is unwise for me to say this. It sounds noble, but people might say it cannot possibly be true. But I guarantee you—it is true. I am not concerned for my own nobility. I am concerned that you understand the life God offers inside the most holy place.

Inside the most holy place, we cannot lose. We are so utterly dependent on God's sovereignty and so fully aware of our responsibility to serve Him that everything makes sense. Nothing dissuades us of that core belief. From the point of view of our purpose in life, nothing bad can happen to us.

Let's say Muslim terrorists kill us because we proclaim Christ. That's not bad.

Let's say the economy crashes and we spend the rest of our lives working at 7-11 and volunteering at the soup kitchen. That's not bad.

Let's say we have everything taken away and we die among desperate people in a snowstorm. That's not bad.

When we are His, everything in life is an opportunity to be faithful and honorable. When we are His, we live lives of extreme availability.

Opportunities We Don't Deserve

Tonight, I have been asked to host the evening broadcast of *Praise the Lord* on the Trinity Broadcasting Network (TBN). I am in a hotel room resting just before the car comes to take me to the studio. As we were putting the program together, I was so grateful to be able to serve. I do not need this program. I do not have anything to sell. I do not have a mailing list to build, speaking dates to fill, an itinerary to complete, or a cause for which to campaign. Instead, I was asked to host and I am doing it. Why? To complement the calling of TBN.

I want to serve TBN and its viewers. They may never have me back, or they might want me to do some additional programs. I hope they will want me back because that would be an indicator that I had served them effectively, but whether or not they have me back is not the purpose of tonight's program. I do not need to be seen. I do not need to succeed for my ministry or for me. But I do need to serve.

Right now, I have the honor of serving as the pastor of New Life Church. New Life is my life's call, and I am so grateful that so many thousands of people have chosen to join with us to worship and study the Scriptures. I am also grateful for every staff member, small group leader, trustee, elder, and friend who has chosen to join with us to train others in biblical principles.

One of the greatest honors in my life is to stand at the podium on Sundays and teach the Bible. I also love staff meetings on Wednesday and trustees' and elders' meetings on Sunday afternoons. Sunday night is great because it is cozier; that is when New Life most feels like a family. In all these things, I love serving as the pastor of New Life Church.

But the day might come when it is no longer right for me to be the senior pastor. I would still serve, one way or another. I would joyfully answer the phone, mow the grass, vacuum the carpets, cuddle with babies in the nursery, or change light bulbs in the World Prayer Center. If for some reason they didn't want me doing those things, I could still pray and serve—happily and gratefully.

My roles do not define me. My income does not give me dignity. I am a most holy place guy. I have settled my issues. I am sold on God's work in the earth in all its forms. I want to faithfully serve every day.

Gayle and I watch Christian people suffer unnecessarily because they have not settled these issues. We have friends who have lost everything and are sad about it. Why? If we lost everything, we would go to the local shopping center, get a job, and support ourselves as best we could. We would live within our means and help others live their lives well.

We have watched some of our friends lose their jobs in ministry and fight to maintain their homes (and what they perceive to be their dignity). We have seen them try to find replacement work in "ministry" that will replace their income and use their expertise. I just do not understand that mentality. Those people need to settle three things:

1. You are always in ministry no matter what you are doing.

2. No one can pay a true minister to minister.

3. This world is not our home.

If you are in this position, there is no reason to be unforgiving, hateful, angry, or sad. Forgive. Faithfully serve every day. Life will work. God is faithful. God wants people He can use. We should develop our skills, add value to our lives, and make sure that we add value to the lives of those who come into contact with us. Whether we live or we die, we joyfully and wisely serve. We don't serve for earthly rewards, even though God wants to give them. We serve because of Him.

That's the most holy place. That's the good life.

I hope you see that these concepts are not difficult to understand, and they are not only for those who can think in hyper-spiritual terms. The good life isn't a far-fetched idea. It is a place of grounding. It is where you are ready, able, and willing. Your eyes are open. Your heart is prepared. Your mind is sharp. You are a competent Christian, and God wants to delight in you and use you every day.

Enjoy the good life. It is the life you are meant to live.

Instructions for the Tabernacle

God's detailed plans for building the tabernacle and the various items within it, along with His instructions for priestly garments and duties, are recorded in Exodus 25–30, as follows:

The Ark of the Covenant

Have them make a chest of acacia wood—two and a half cubits long, a cubit and a half wide, and a cubit and a half high. Overlay it with pure gold, both inside and out, and make a gold molding around it. Cast four gold rings for it and fasten them to its four feet, with two rings on one side and two rings on the other. Then make poles of acacia wood and overlay them with gold. Insert the poles into the rings on the sides of the chest to carry it. The poles are to remain in the rings of this ark; they are not to be removed. Then put in the ark the Testimony, which I will give you.

Make an atonement cover of pure gold—two and a half cubits long and a cubit and a half wide. And make two cherubim out of hammered gold at the ends of the cover. Make one cherub on one end and the second cherub on the other; make the cherubim of one piece with the cover, at the two ends. The cherubim are to have their wings spread upward, overshadowing the cover with them. The cherubim are to face each other, looking toward the cover. Place the cover on top of the ark and put in the ark the Testimony, which I will give you. There, above the cover between the two cherubim that are over the ark of the Testimony, I will meet with you and give you all my commands for the Israelites.

—Exodus 25:10–22

The Table and the Bread of the Presence

Make a table of acacia wood—two cubits long, a cubit wide and a cubit and a half high. Overlay it with pure gold and make a gold molding around it. Also make around it a rim a handbreadth wide and put a gold molding on the rim. Make four gold rings for the table and fasten them to the four corners, where the four legs are. The rings are to be close to the rim to hold the poles used in carrying the table. Make the poles of acacia wood, overlay them with gold and carry the table with them. And make its plates and dishes of pure gold, as well as its pitchers and bowls for the pouring out of offerings. Put the bread of the Presence on this table to be before me at all times.

—Exodus 25:23–30

The Lampstand

Make a lampstand of pure gold and hammer it out, base and shaft; its flowerlike cups, buds and blossoms shall be of one piece with it. Six branches are to extend from the sides of the lampstand—three on one side and three on the other. Three cups shaped like almond flowers with buds and blossoms are to be on one branch, three on the next branch, and the same for all six branches extending from the lampstand. And on the lampstand there are to be four cups shaped like almond flowers with buds and blossoms. One bud shall be under the first pair of branches extending from the lampstand, a second bud under the second pair, and a third bud under the third pair—six branches in all. The buds and branches shall all be of one piece with the lampstand, hammered out of pure gold.

Then make its seven lamps and set them up on it so that they light the space in front of it. Its wick trimmers and trays are to be of pure gold. A talent of pure gold is to be used for the lampstand and all these accessories. See that you make them according to the pattern shown you on the mountain.

—Exodus 25:31–40

The Tabernacle

Make the tabernacle with ten curtains of finely twisted linen and blue, purple and scarlet yarn, with cherubim worked into them by a skilled craftsman. All the curtains are to be the same size—twenty-eight cubits long and four cubits wide. Join five of the curtains together, and do the same with the other five. Make loops of blue material along the edge of the end curtain in one set, and do the same with the end curtain in the other set. Make fifty loops on one curtain and fifty loops on the end curtain of the other set, with the loops opposite each other. Then make fifty gold clasps and use them to fasten the curtains together so that the tabernacle is a unit.

Make curtains of goat hair for the tent over the tabernacle—eleven altogether. All eleven curtains are to be the same size—thirty cubits long and four cubits wide. Join five of the curtains together into one set and the other six into another set. Fold the sixth curtain double at the front of the tent. Make fifty loops along the edge of the end curtain in one set and also along the edge of the end curtain in the other set. Then make fifty bronze clasps and put them in the loops to fasten the tent together as a unit. As for the additional length of the tent curtains, the half curtain that is left over is to hang down at the rear of the taber-nacle. The tent curtains will be a cubit longer on both sides; what is left will hang over the sides of the tabernacle so as to cover it. Make for the tent a covering of ram skins dyed red, and over that a covering of hides of sea cows.

Make upright frames of acacia wood for the tabernacle. Each frame is to be ten cubits long and a cubit and a half wide, with two projections set parallel to each other. Make all the frames of the tabernacle in this way. Make twenty frames for the south side of the tabernacle and make forty silver bases to go under them—two bases for each frame, one under each projection. For the other side, the north side of the tabernacle, make twenty frames and forty silver bases—two under each frame. Make six frames for the far end, that is, the west end of the tabernacle, and make two frames for the corners at the far end. At these two corners they must be double from the bottom all the way to the top, and fitted into a single ring; both shall be like that. So there will be eight frames and sixteen silver bases—two under each frame.

Also make crossbars of acacia wood: five for the frames on one side of the tabernacle, five for those on the other side, and five for the frames on the west, at the far end of the tabernacle. The center crossbar is to extend from end to end at the middle of the frames. Overlay the frames with gold and make gold rings to hold the crossbars. Also overlay the crossbars with gold.

Set up the tabernacle according to the plan shown you on the mountain.   —Exodus 26:1–30

The Veil

Make a curtain of blue, purple and scarlet yarn and finely twisted linen, with cherubim worked into it by a skilled craftsman. Hang it with gold hooks on four posts of acacia wood overlaid with gold and standing on four silver bases. Hang the curtain from the clasps and place the ark of the Testimony behind the curtain. The curtain will separate the Holy Place from the Most Holy Place. Put the atonement cover on the ark of the Testimony in the Most Holy Place. Place the table outside the curtain on the north side of the tabernacle and put the lampstand opposite it on the south side.

For the entrance to the tent make a curtain of blue, purple and scarlet yarn and finely twisted linen—the work of an embroiderer. Make gold hooks for this curtain and five posts of acacia wood overlaid with gold. And cast five bronze bases for them.

—Exodus 26:31–37

The Bronze Altar

Build an altar of acacia wood, three cubits high; it is to be square, five cubits long and five cubits wide. Make a horn at each of the four corners, so that the horns and the altar are of one piece, and overlay the altar with bronze. Make all its utensils of bronze—its pots to remove the ashes, and its shovels, sprinkling bowls, meat forks and firepans. Make a grating for it, a bronze network, and make a bronze ring at each of the four corners of the network. Put it under the ledge of the altar so that it is halfway up the altar. Make poles of acacia wood for the altar and overlay them with bronze. The poles are to be inserted into the rings so they will be on two sides of the altar when it is carried. Make the altar hollow, out of boards. It is to be made just as you were shown on the mountain.

—Exodus 27:1–8

The Outer Court

Make a courtyard for the tabernacle. The south side shall be a hundred cubits long and is to have curtains of finely twisted linen, with twenty posts and twenty bronze bases and with silver hooks and bands on the posts. The north side shall also be a hundred cubits long and is to have curtains, with twenty posts and twenty bronze bases and with silver hooks and bands on the posts.

The west end of the courtyard shall be fifty cubits wide and have curtains, with ten posts and ten bases. On the east end, toward the sunrise, the courtyard shall also be fifty cubits wide. Curtains fifteen cubits long are to be on one side of the entrance, with three posts and three bases, and curtains fifteen cubits long are to be on the other side, with three posts and three bases.

For the entrance to the courtyard, provide a curtain twenty cubits long, of blue, purple and scarlet yarn and finely twisted linen—the work of an embroiderer—with four posts and four bases. All the posts around the courtyard are to have silver bands and hooks, and bronze bases. The courtyard shall be a hundred cubits long and fifty cubits wide, with curtains of finely twisted linen five cubits high, and with bronze bases. All the other articles used in the service of the tabernacle, whatever their function, including all the tent pegs for it and those for the courtyard, are to be of bronze.

—Exodus 27:9–19

Oil for the Lampstand

Command the Israelites to bring you clear oil of pressed olives for the light so that the lamps may be kept burning. In the Tent of Meeting, outside the curtain that is in front of the Testimony, Aaron and his sons are to keep the lamps burning before the LORD from evening till morning. This is to be a lasting ordinance among the Israelites for the generations to come.

—Exodus 27:20–21

The Priestly Garments

Have Aaron your brother brought to you from among the Israelites, along with his sons Nadab and Abihu, Eleazar and Ithamar, so they may serve me as priests. Make sacred garments for your brother Aaron, to give him dignity and honor. Tell all the skilled men to whom I have given wisdom in such matters that they are to make garments for Aaron, for his consecration, so he may serve me as priest. These are the garments they are to make: a breastpiece, an ephod, a robe, a woven tunic, a turban and a sash. They are to make these sacred garments for your brother Aaron and his sons, so they may serve me as priests. Have them use gold, and blue, purple and scarlet yarn, and fine linen.

—Exodus 28:1–5

The Ephod

Make the ephod of gold, and of blue, purple and scarlet yarn, and of finely twisted linen—the work of a skilled craftsman. It is to have two shoulder pieces attached to two of its corners, so it can be fastened. Its skillfully woven waistband is to be like it—of one piece with the ephod and made with gold, and with blue, purple and scarlet yarn, and with finely twisted linen.

Take two onyx stones and engrave on them the names of the sons of Israel in the order of their birth—six names on one stone and the remaining six on the other. Engrave the names of the sons of Israel on the two stones the way a gem cutter engraves a seal. Then mount the stones in gold filigree settings and fasten them on the shoulder pieces of the ephod as memorial stones for the sons of Israel. Aaron is to bear the names on his shoulders as a memorial before the LORD. Make gold filigree settings and two braided chains of pure gold, like a rope, and attach the chains to the settings.

—Exodus 28:6–14

The Breastpiece

Fashion a breastpiece for making decisions—the work of a skilled craftsman. Make it like the ephod: of gold, and of blue, purple and scarlet yarn, and of finely twisted linen. It is to be square—a span long and a span wide—and folded double. Then mount four rows of precious stones on it. In the first row there shall be a ruby, a topaz and a beryl; in the second row a turquoise, a sapphire and an emerald; in the third row a jacinth, an agate and an amethyst; in the fourth row a chrysolite, an onyx and a jasper. Mount them in gold filigree settings. There are to be twelve stones, one for each of the names of the sons of Israel, each engraved like a seal with the name of one of the twelve tribes.

For the breastpiece make braided chains of pure gold, like a rope. Make two gold rings for it and fasten them to two corners of the breastpiece. Fasten the two gold chains to the rings at the corners of the breastpiece, and the other ends of the chains to the two settings, attaching them to the shoulder pieces of the ephod at the front. Make two gold rings and attach them to the other two corners of the breastpiece on the inside edge next to the ephod. Make two more gold rings and attach them to the bottom of the shoulder pieces on the front of the ephod, close to the seam just above the waistband of the ephod. The rings of the breastpiece are to be tied to the rings of the ephod with blue cord, connecting it to the waistband, so that the breastpiece will not swing out from the ephod.

Whenever Aaron enters the Holy Place, he will bear the names of the sons of Israel over his heart on the breastpiece of decision as a continuing memorial before the LORD. Also put the Urim and the Thummim in the breastpiece, so they may be over Aaron's heart whenever he enters the presence of the LORD. Thus Aaron will always bear the means of making decisions for the Israelites over his heart before the LORD.   —Exodus 28:15–30

Other Priestly Garments

Make the robe of the ephod entirely of blue cloth, with an opening for the head in its center. There shall be a woven edge like a collar around this opening, so that it will not tear. Make pomegranates of blue, purple and scarlet yarn around the hem of the robe, with gold bells between them. The gold bells and the pomegranates are to alternate around the hem of the robe. Aaron must wear it when he ministers. The sound of the bells will be heard when he enters the Holy Place before the LORD and when he comes out, so that he will not die.

Make a plate of pure gold and engrave on it as on a seal: HOLY TO THE LORD. Fasten a blue cord to it to attach it to the turban; it is to be on the front of the turban. It will be on Aaron's forehead, and he will bear the guilt involved in the sacred gifts the Israelites consecrate, whatever their gifts may be. It will be on Aaron's forehead continually so that they will be acceptable to the LORD.

Weave the tunic of fine linen and make the turban of fine linen. The sash is to be the work of an embroiderer. Make tunics, sashes and headbands for Aaron's sons, to give them dignity and honor. After you put these clothes on your brother Aaron and his sons, anoint and ordain them. Consecrate them so they may serve me as priests.

Make linen undergarments as a covering for the body, reaching from the waist to the thigh. Aaron and his sons must wear them whenever they enter the Tent of Meeting or approach the altar to minister in the Holy Place, so that they will not incur guilt and die.

This is to be a lasting ordinance for Aaron and his descendants.

—Exodus 28:31–43

Consecration of the Priests

This is what you are to do to consecrate them, so they may serve me as priests: Take a young bull and two rams without defect. And from fine wheat flour, without yeast, make bread, and cakes mixed with oil, and wafers spread with oil. Put them in a basket and present them in it—along with the bull and the two rams. Then bring Aaron and his sons to the entrance to the Tent of Meeting and wash them with water. Take the garments and dress Aaron with the tunic, the robe of the ephod, the ephod itself and the breastpiece. Fasten the ephod on him by its skillfully woven waistband. Put the turban on his head and attach the sacred diadem to the turban. Take the anointing oil and anoint him by pouring it on his head. Bring his sons and dress them in tunics and put headbands on them. Then tie sashes on Aaron and his sons. The priesthood is theirs by a lasting ordinance. In this way you shall ordain Aaron and his sons.

Bring the bull to the front of the Tent of Meeting, and Aaron and his sons shall lay their hands on its head. Slaughter it in the LORD's presence at the entrance to the Tent of Meeting. Take some of the bull's blood and put it on the horns of the altar with your finger, and pour out the rest of it at the base of the altar. Then take all the fat around the inner parts, the covering of the liver, and both kidneys with the fat on them, and burn them on the altar. But burn the bull's flesh and its hide and its offal outside the camp. It is a sin offering.

Take one of the rams, and Aaron and his sons shall lay their hands on its head. Slaughter it and take the blood and sprinkle it against the altar on all sides. Cut the ram into pieces and wash the inner parts and the legs, putting them with the head and the other pieces. Then burn the entire ram on the altar. It is a burnt offering to the LORD, a pleasing aroma, an offering made to the LORD by fire.

Take the other ram, and Aaron and his sons shall lay their hands on its head. Slaughter it, take some of its blood and put it on the lobes of the right ears of Aaron and his sons, on the thumbs of their right hands, and on the big toes of their right feet. Then sprinkle blood against the altar on all sides. And take some of the blood on the altar and some of the anointing oil and sprinkle it on Aaron and his garments and on his sons and their garments. Then he and his sons and their garments will be consecrated.

Take from this ram the fat, the fat tail, the fat around the inner parts, the covering of the liver, both kidneys with the fat on them, and the right thigh. (This is the ram for the ordination.) From the basket of bread made without yeast, which is before the LORD, take a loaf, and a cake made with oil, and a wafer. Put all these in the hands of Aaron and his sons and wave them before the LORD as a wave offering. Then take them from their hands and burn them on the altar along with the burnt offering for a pleasing aroma to the LORD, an offering made to the LORD by fire. After you take the breast of the ram for Aaron's ordination, wave it before the LORD as a wave offering, and it will be your share.

Consecrate those parts of the ordination ram that belong to Aaron and his sons: the breast that was waved and the thigh that was presented. This is always to be the regular share from the Israelites for Aaron and his sons. It is the contribution the Israelites are to make to the LORD from their fellowship offerings.

Aaron's sacred garments will belong to his descendants so that they can be anointed and ordained in them. The son who succeeds him as priest and comes to the Tent of Meeting to minister in the Holy Place is to wear them seven days.

Take the ram for the ordination and cook the meat in a sacred place. At the entrance to the Tent of Meeting, Aaron and his sons are to eat the meat of the ram and the bread that is in the basket. They are to eat these offerings by which atonement was made for their ordination and consecration. But no one else may eat them, because they are sacred. And if any of the meat of the ordination ram or any bread is left over till morning, burn it up. It must not be eaten, because it is sacred.

Do for Aaron and his sons everything I have commanded you, taking seven days to ordain them. Sacrifice a bull each day as a sin offering to make atonement. Purify the altar by making atonement for it, and anoint it to consecrate it. For seven days make atonement for the altar and consecrate it. Then the altar will be most holy, and whatever touches it will be holy.

This is what you are to offer on the altar regularly each day: two lambs a year old. Offer one in the morning and the other at twilight. With the first lamb offer a tenth of an ephah of fine flour mixed with a quarter of a hin of oil from pressed olives, and a quarter of a hin of wine as a drink offering. Sacrifice the other lamb at twilight with the same grain offering and its drink offering as in the morning—a pleasing aroma, an offering made to the LORD by fire.

For the generations to come this burnt offering is to be made regularly at the entrance to the Tent of Meeting before the LORD. There I will meet you and speak to you; there also I will meet with the Israelites, and the place will be consecrated by my glory.

So I will consecrate the Tent of Meeting and the altar and will consecrate Aaron and his sons to serve me as priests. Then I will dwell among the Israelites and be their God. They will know that I am the LORD their God, who brought them out of Egypt so that I might dwell among them. I am the LORD their God.

—Exodus 29:1–46

The Altar of Incense

Make an altar of acacia wood for burning incense. It is to be square, a cubit long and a cubit wide, and two cubits high—its horns of one piece with it. Overlay the top and all the sides and the horns with pure gold, and make a gold molding around it. Make two gold rings for the altar below the molding—two on opposite sides—to hold the poles used to carry it. Make the poles of acacia wood and overlay them with gold. Put the altar in front of the curtain that is before the ark of the Testimony—before the atonement cover that is over the Testimony—where I will meet with you.

Aaron must burn fragrant incense on the altar every morning when he tends the lamps. He must burn incense again when he lights the lamps at twilight so incense will burn regularly before the LORD for the generations to come. Do not offer on this altar any other incense or any burnt offering or grain offering, and do not pour a drink offering on it. Once a year Aaron shall make atonement on its horns. This annual atonement must be made with the blood of the atoning sin offering for the generations to come. It is most holy to the LORD.

—Exodus 30:1–10

The Bronze Basin

Then the LORD said to Moses, "Make a bronze basin, with its bronze stand, for washing. Place it between the Tent of Meeting and the altar, and put water in it. Aaron and his sons are to wash their hands and feet with water from it. Whenever they enter the Tent of Meeting, they shall wash with water so that they will not die. Also, when they approach the altar to minister by presenting an offering made to the LORD by fire, they shall wash their hands and feet so that they will not die. This is to be a lasting ordinance for Aaron and his descendants for the generations to come."

—Exodus 30:17–21

Anointing Oil

Then the LORD said to Moses, "Take the following fine spices: 500 shekels of liquid myrrh, half as much (that is, 250 shekels) of fragrant cinnamon, 250 shekels of fragrant cane, 500 shekels of cassia—all according to the sanctuary shekel—and a hin of olive oil. Make these into a sacred anointing oil, a fragrant blend, the work of a perfumer. It will be the sacred anointing oil. Then use it to anoint the Tent of Meeting, the ark of the Testimony, the table and all its articles, the lampstand and its accessories, the altar of incense, the altar of burnt offering and all its utensils, and the basin with its stand. You shall consecrate them so they will be most holy, and whatever touches them will be holy.

"Anoint Aaron and his sons and consecrate them so they may serve me as priests. Say to the Israelites, 'This is to be my sacred anointing oil for the generations to come. Do not pour it on men's bodies and do not make any oil with the same formula. It is sacred, and you are to consider it sacred. Whoever makes perfume like it and whoever puts it on anyone other than a priest must be cut off from his people.'"

—Exodus 30:22–33

Incense

Then the LORD said to Moses, "Take fragrant spices—gum resin, onycha and galbanum—and pure frankincense, all in equal amounts, and make a fragrant blend of incense, the work of a perfumer. It is to be salted and pure and sacred. Grind some of it to powder and place it in front of the Testimony in the Tent of Meeting, where I will meet with you. It shall be most holy to you. Do not make any incense with this formula for yourselves; consider it holy to the LORD. Whoever makes any like it to enjoy its fragrance must be cut off from his people."

—Exodus 30:34–38

OTHER RESOURCES BY AUTHOR

Books

The Life Giving Church

Dog Training, Fly Fishing, and
Sharing Christ in the 21st Century

Simple Prayers for a Powerful Life

Letters From Home

Loving Your City Into the Kingdom

Taking It to the Streets

Confident Parents, Exceptional Teens (with John Bolin)

Foolish No More!

The Jerusalem Diet

Booklets

Who's in Charge Here

So You Want to Get Married

No More Lonely Nights

Fraud in the Storehouse

How to Take Authority Over Your Mind, Home,
Business and Country

Liberation Through Prayer and Fasting

Freedom Through Forgiveness

Free Enterprise

Teaching Series (CDs)

A Place to Worship

The S Series (Suicide, Sexual Purity, Suffering, Satan)

The Providence of God

Videos

Loving Your City Into the Kingdom
Prayerwalking Your City
Primary Purpose

To order these resources or for further information, contact:

New Life Church
11025 Voyager Parkway
Colorado Springs, CO 80921
Phone: (719) 594-6602

Web sites:
www.newlifechurch.org
www.tedhaggard.com

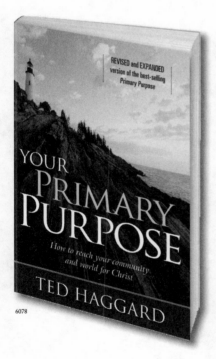